Advice From
A 90-Year-Old Man

*Life Lessons
For Happiness and Prosperity*

By Steve Mucha

*Good luck in life.
Steve Mucha*

Improverbial Books

Advice from a 90-Year-Old Man

ISBN: 978-0-9890774-0-8

Copyright © 2013

All rights reserved, including the right of reproduction in whole or in part of any form.

This book is not intended to substitute for professional financial advice. Always consult a financial professional before making a major investment or money decision.

Improverbial Books
7 Ninth Avenue
Haddon Heights, NJ 08035
www.improverbial.com

On the cover:
Author Steve Mucha and his wife, Carol Copper

To Carol, my Adaptable Idealist

and Musical Muse.

And to grandchildren everywhere,

the hope of the future.

Table of Contents

Introduction: I Learned a Lot in 90 Years   3

PART 1: LESSONS FROM HARD TIMES
1. The Deadly Sled   7
2. My Parents' Financial Philosophy   11
3. My Big Brothers   15
4. Our Family's Store   19
5. Movie Dishes and 100 Fishes   23

PART 2: MONEY LESSONS FOR TODAY
6. Hard Knocks and Recession Socks   31
7. Popcorn and a Soda Retirement Plan   35
8. Starting a Retirement Plan   41
9. Thoughts About Investing   47
10. Better Late Than Never   51
11. Mortgage Management   55
12. Career Advice: Earning and Learning   57
13. Too Good to Be True   63

PART 3: LIFE LESSONS FROM NINE DECADES
14. A Few Tips About Marriage   69
15. Second Chances and Second Best   77
16. A Better Cup of Coffee   83
17. My Great Golf Idea   85
18. I Remember My Children   91
19. Musical Muses   97
20. Just for Laughs: Some Favorite Jokes   101
21. On Growing Older   105

About the Author   110

INTRODUCTION

I Learned a Lot in 90 Years

Experience is a costly teacher, and it sometimes comes too late. You wind up paying for your lack of perspective again and again. You say to yourself, "If I'd only known this before, I would have done things differently and I would have been better off."

By the time I got to be 87 years old, when I started writing this book, I had learned so many things. Often, I wished I had learned my lessons earlier — when I was 25 or 35 or even 50 years old. The insights could have helped.

A strange and interesting thing is that life always seems to give us another choice worth considering. Can you imagine what you could do if you were able to think of two extra options? You would make smarter and faster decisions. Soon you would realize that just going and doing something without thinking is far from the wisest course.

Even if an alternative comes from someone else's experience, perhaps from a book like this, it gives you one extra option. You gain that knowledge, without having to experience it yourself. And once you know it, it will be there, ready for your use now and in the future. Such a step takes your life out of the minimum choice of yes or no. Don't limit yourself to just yes or no. Decisions like that are too easy to regret later.

Now if you were able to add three extra options, you could be the boss.

That's why I wrote this book. I hoped to stimulate others and help them to think and do without having to learn only from their own experience. That's the hard way, especially later in life.

I'm no millionaire, and I was never a bigshot politician. My life story probably sounds like the lives of many Americans. I was born in 1921 and grew up in Carteret, New Jersey, a working class town across from Staten Island with many immigrants at the time. My parents came over from Czechoslovakia before meeting here, getting married, and starting a family. My two brothers and I served in World War II, and I met my first wife while going to Swarthmore College to earn an engineering degree on the G.I. Bill. To help raise four children, mostly in the Philadelphia suburbs, I took a career path from designing photographic printing equipment to selling it, then from being a sales manager to starting a business as a manufacturer's representative. I always loved photography, golf and music. Remarriage and retirement brought lots of new adventures. It may not have been a glamorous life, but it's been a good one!

In those ninety years, I believe I learned a lot that others might want to know. I especially hope to help people get started on saving for their futures. In the last few decades, many individuals and families have dropped the conservative "save money now" habit and replaced it with "buy now and pay later." As a result, we fell into perilous times, with some businesses closing and many laying off workers. "Buy now and pay later" isn't working anymore.

Please understand. I am 90 years old, and like so many of us seniors, have had strokes, a heart bypass, arthritis and other health problems. I take many medications, exercise and just keep working at it, trying to get along each day.

This is not a textbook. I can't give you all the answers you would like to have. Just some helpful suggestions that worked for me over the years.

I just want to pass them on.

Steve Mucha

PART 1

LESSONS LEARNED IN HARD TIMES

The author's parents on their wedding day, about 1914.

CHAPTER 1

The Deadly Sled

In the late 1920s, near the start of the Great Depression, WOR, an AM radio station, set up a new broadcast tower just a few miles outside of Carteret, New Jersey, where we lived. Everyone in town was excited. The powerful signal would make our small and weak radios work better and louder.

I was about seven years old, the youngest of three brothers. John, the oldest, was named after our father, who was a union carpenter. Paul was the one who told me all about being able to hear WOR on a crystal set.

"What's a crystal set?" I asked.

Paul made a diagram and explained how it worked. I told a buddy, and we went out along the railroad tracks looking for crystals and small pieces of wood approximately three inches square and a half-inch thick. Paul had a roll of thin copper wire. You mounted the crystal on the wood soldered to a piece of the copper wire, which was connected to a cheap single earphone. You also made a coil by wrapping a single layer of wire around a wooden thread spool, with extra wire for an antenna. A loose wire from the crystal was used to scratch on the coil, the way of locating WOR.

And yes, WOR came in loud and clear. It was great! You could listen to news and music, and I especially liked science-fiction and other adventure stories. I built bunches of these very basic crystal sets and sold them to the neighborhood kids for three cents each, the price of a newspaper. But you had to provide your own earphone, which everybody seemed to have.

That's the way things were back then. You made your own fun, which could mean a little work, but even more satisfaction.

On summer days, as we boys walked along the railroad tracks, just walking and talking and throwing stones, we would stop off for a swim in a creek. We just jumped in the water without bathing suits or anything else on. Every time a train came, we made sure that we were in the water, waving our hands at everybody while it went by. Then we would climb out and sit in the sun to talk and to dry, and then put our clothes back on and go home. You will never convince me that this wasn't more fun with more and better exercise than sitting on a couch playing video games. We also got a good amount of sun and Vitamin D.

We were always busy. Walking. Talking. Or playing baseball with a ball that always needed sewing together at the seams, which we were good at. Baseball gloves were scarce. There were only a couple on the block. You had to get good at catching barehanded. Even those outfield fly balls. Bats were always broken and then taped, only to be broken and taped again. One time, the kids talked me into being the catcher. It was fun. I liked it. I liked those close calls at home plate, tagging the runner out. What made me give up being the catcher were the foul balls bouncing off my head. Nobody had a mask, and it hurt. It only took one shiner, and my mother said, "No more playing catcher." I went back into the outfield.

A football was a luxury. In our neighborhood, there were only two or three footballs, and none of good quality. If somebody had one, it was treated with care. It had to be, or it wouldn't last. A half-dozen or more boys would get together to play touch or tackle football. Touch on barren dirt fields. Tackle on grassy fields. Fortunately, a couple of neighbors had grassy fields that were next to their homes, and actually let us play there. After we played, we would go and sit on big rocks in a circle in the dirt field and tell stories, about adventures that someone had heard. We even got pretty good at making up our own stories to tell. Imagination was boundless.

At campfires at night on fields in the neighborhood, you could hear some pretty scary ghost stories that were told with verve and acted out to make them even scarier. Little brothers always came with a bigger brother to sit close to.

Of the approximately 30 kids in our neighborhood, only one was obese. All the others were trim and very active. How does that compare with today?

In the winter, we would go sliding across the frozen pond that was two blocks away. Or we would go ice skating with our skates, which were the kind you strapped onto your shoes. They were tough to put on and even tougher to use. When you fell, which was often, they got loose again.

One day, when I was seven or eight years old, we were playing "I dare you to sled over the ice hole!" The hole was small, and it was no problem, until one boy started to chop the hole bigger. We couldn't quit now! So we all ran and sledded fast over the bigger hole. Then the hole in the ice got pretty big. Everybody was teasing everybody else to try the larger hole. So yours truly said, "I'll give it a try!" I ran fast with my sled, dove on it, came up to the hole, and the sled and I just went right in — under the ice. It happened so fast. I remember being scared, cold, shocked and determined to do two things. First, don't breathe! Second, don't let go of the family sled!

All that was left above the ice were my ankles and shoes. Fortunately for me, they were quickly grabbed by my buddies, who yanked me out feet first. I still had that sled in my hands. I'd get spanked if I lost it.

When I got home I was soaked and freezing, and my mother pulled off my wet icy clothes, dried me, put dry clothes on me, and wrapped a blanket around me. Only then did she burst into tears.

Then she sat me down and did something she probably learned growing up in Eastern Europe. She and my dad grew up in neighboring towns in what became Czechoslovakia. They only met, however, after they moved to America before World War I. My mother got a glass of water, and lit a wooden match. After it burned halfway, she switched fingers to the burned end and held the unburned end upright until the whole matchstick burned out. I was engrossed at what I was seeing. Then she dropped the match in the glass of water. It sizzled. She handed me the glass and said, "Drink the water."

I looked at the match floating in the water and then I looked up at my mother and said, "Momma, are we witches?"

But I know the idea wasn't to ward off evil spirits. Supposedly, the burned match gave off some chemical that was good for you.

Oh yes, because of the near-catastrophe, I got scolded for days. But not spanked. She also hugged me many times over the next few days.

The day after the incident, when I went out to play, my friends who played the sled-over-the-ice-hole game all treated me with extra respect. Only my brothers called me "stupid."

One extra thing about WOR: Early on, a mystifying problem started occurring. The newspaper wrote about it: "WOR plays music from man's mouth while he sleeps." Some people in our town were playing the sounds and programs of WOR just by opening their mouths! They were walking radio sets. It turned out that fillings in teeth caused some of this magical development. "A walking radio set," was how the Daily News described it. Almost everybody in Carteret was talking about it. Then it happened to me. I had a cavity. The dentist filled it. I started to get complaints from my family to shut my mouth when I was sleeping. "It's noisy with WOR music," they said. About 10 days later, it stopped. I had no explanation. We were all mystified as to how it would come and go differently with people. But it was exciting for a while. One burly man, somebody's uncle, claimed to have the biggest volume. His family, though, didn't share his enthusiasm during the nights. Then it became old hat, and nobody wanted to hear about it anymore.

See, you can have a happy, busy life without a lot of money or toys. You just need ingenuity and a sense of adventure — and friends to grab your ankles when your sled goes under the ice.

CHAPTER 2

My Parents' Financial Philosophy

It's tough to put money away to just save it. Especially when you are only 20 or 30 or even 40 years old. It's just too easy to adopt the philosophy to spend now and save later. When you see things advertised on TV and everywhere you look, you're tempted to think: "There are so many things I need to buy. My friends have them, so why shouldn't I?" So you don't put money away now, but plan to do it later. Besides, what's the big deal?

What a far cry from my parents' philosophy. They lived during the Great Depression, which historians say began with the stock market crash in 1929 and lasted about a decade in the United States. I was born in 1921, so I was eight years old when the Great Depression started. When it hit, life was tough. We didn't have extra money. Food was scarce. Jobs were scarce. My brothers and I each got one toy for Christmas. They were handmade by my father from left-over wood. But they were great toys, good enough to pass on to our children in later years.

My father would go out on Christmas Eve and find a left-over Christmas tree that was broken and being discarded because it didn't sell. He'd buy it cheap and bring it home, and we were happy to dress up that wounded tree. My mother baked her Czechoslovakian family recipe foods and cookies, and we would have a joyous Christmastime. We didn't have much, but our parents saw to it that love and happiness were in our home.

My parents met as teenagers after they came to the United States from Czechoslovakia, where they grew up about five miles apart. They got married around 1914. They taught me about saving money. They practiced the philosophy of the times, which was to save every bit you can, invest it at the best interest rate you can find, and then let it grow. With interest, it grew slowly, but they knew it would be there later.

That's a basic difference between then and now: conservative saving vs. the modern idea of "have and enjoy it now — we'll save later." This has been a very popular attitude. But the last 30 years have shown that this approach is not working. Less retirement money will be available if you spend and enjoy your money now. The old folks were glad to have the money later in retirement. They just figured that saving was a good move. Do you? Have you learned how to stretch your dollars so that you can save some now?

When I was a little boy, one of my brothers or I would have to run the same errand on Fridays after school. It was to take money to the local money lender to make a minimum weekly mortgage payment on what my parents owed. (The bank didn't lend the money.) He lived many blocks away and I would walk over to his house, knock on the door, and tell him, "Here are the payment book and this week's payment." It was in cash, and I would watch him count the money, including a week's interest. Then he would enter the amount in the payment book. He would add it up, sign the new reduced balance, always smile, and say, "Your mother and father are good people, and tell them I wish them good health." I would say, "Thank you," and as I walked home, I noticed that in my parent's payment record book, the balance decreased a little every week. It took eight years of weekly payments until this ten-year mortgage was all paid off, and my parents threw a party to celebrate. I always remembered that you had to pay all the weekly interest that you owed, and pay it before any of the mortgage balance was deducted. Sometimes my parents would pay a little extra and would say to each other, "If we can pay it off faster, then we won't have to pay any extra interest." They didn't like paying interest. To them, it was your own money that you couldn't spend, because you had to give it to somebody else. I always remembered this advice, and they didn't even go past fifth grade in school. They knew it just wasn't smart to have to pay extra interest. To them, it was just plain wasteful.

But I must say something about the local money lender man. He loaned my parents more money to add a store in the space that was previously occupied by our living room, my parents' bedroom and a hallway. The year was 1928, and I was seven years old. My brother Paul was nine, and John was eleven. After the Depression hit in 1929, a few times we couldn't pay anything, and some weeks we couldn't pay much at all. The lender man never said, "You didn't make a full payment this month, so I am foreclosing." Even when we didn't pay much, Mr. Schwartz would still say, "Your mother and father are good people, and I wish them good health." He never said anything in a critical or demeaning way. That's why I respected him. When I got home and handed the mortgage book to my parents, they would ask, "What did he say?" And I would tell them. They would say something like, "He is a good man. We are lucky that he loaned us the money." These were indeed bad Depression times, when many people understood what was going on and helped others. To us, the money lender man was one of those kind people.

Today's world is so different. Interest is now a popular convenience charge to buy whatever you want and pay for at a later date. The credit card companies have flourished with "Just put a little down and you can have it now!" Buying now and paying later is so easy to do that it can get a hold on you — if you let it. I have seen advertisements claiming that if you buy their product, you can start paying in a year or sometimes two. Seems too good to be true, and often it is! I've also seen articles in the newspapers and comments on TV that the average credit card debt at the time was over $8,000. If your yearly interest rate is 24 percent, that is 2 percent a month, which is $160. For one month. That's almost $2,000 a year! Wow!

Here's a story about my mother in the Depression. Money was scarce. People were selling apples on the street. And yet she managed to save a little here and a little there. These bits totaled up to bringing six family members from Czechoslovakia over to America in an eight-year period. Her measure of love for others was greater than her desire for indulging in using money for her own conveniences. It was her choice. I know six people who thanked her for her choice. I was there. You could tell by their tears and the hugs that they meant it when they called my mother "the little five-foot, ninety-eight-pound giant!" The philosophy of parents often differs from the philosophy of their children and grandchildren. "You are old-fashioned," say a lot of modern children and grandchildren. "You are spending too much," say the parents and grandparents. Yes, two different philosophies.

When I was growing up, not everybody had a car. Most people walked a mile or two to their jobs, and you even repaired or patched your own beat-up shoes if you wanted to keep wearing shoes. My brothers and I were good shoe-repair boys for the family. We didn't complain. We just replaced the heels and patched up the soles with a can of shoe-patch cement that hardened into a black spot on the bottom of your shoes. Sometimes it lasted two or three weeks before it fell off or just got worn out again. And we would fix it again ... and again. The go-without-shoes option was just not talked about.

Shoes were handed down just like clothes. Having two older brothers, I got the best of the deal, because I had more choices. John, my oldest brother, would get some older cousin's shoes. Sometimes, though, he would actually get a new pair.

That was the way of life in the Depression: Pass it on! We were recycling long before Earth Day. If you didn't need it or you outgrew it, somebody else could use it. You would be surprised at how good mothers were at fitting a larger size of clothing to a smaller size to use again. I'm not saying you should fix your own shoes. These days, with mass production, it's often cheaper to buy something new than to fix something old. But learning to do with less, even a little less, is a good habit that can pay off big over the long run. When you dine out, do you order more food than you can eat and then have the server discard it? I have seen a lot of young people do this much too often. My parents would say, "If you didn't buy too much, then money would still be in your pocket. It could even help to pay a bill."

It was a good philosophy in those Depression times.

Can you think of a better philosophy for recession times, or even optimistic times?

CHAPTER 3

My Big Brothers

I had two big brothers: John, who was four years older, and Paul, who was two years older than me. We had no middle names. My parents didn't believe they were necessary. One good one was enough. And so we were John, Paul and Stephen.

John loved music. When he was eight years old, he wanted to play the violin. It was 1925 and times were still good, so my parents bought him one. He took lessons for almost three years, until my father started working fewer hours. John was good almost from the start. He practiced and practiced and just kept on getting better. I can't recall my parents ever telling John to go and practice. He'd just come home from school, pick up the violin and play for a while, even before he did his homework.

I did see my mother and father smile whenever he did practice. John got to be good very fast. By the time he was eleven, he was already playing in a local orchestra. By the time he was twelve, he had started to teach himself to play a used guitar. But the violin was always his first love.

He was soon good enough to start making money playing with a band of grownups. By age 17, he was playing with three bands, and he had saved enough money to buy his own used car to get to his bands' many gigs. I remember how proud he was when he came home with his Chevrolet coupe that had a rumble seat. Paul and I always wanted to ride in the exterior flip-out seat, even if it was raining, because everybody could see us riding with our big brother in his $50 used car. John kept it in good condition, too, with advice and help from our father.

John joined the Army not long before World War II, and after war was declared against Japan, Germany and Italy in December 1941, he was shipped to England, where he serviced fighter planes and bombers.

Paul had his own interests, including tennis and photography. Someone gave him a broken used camera, and he fixed it and started taking pictures. He developed them in the basement at night. My father saw this and offered to help him build a darkroom. Together they built one in the basement. It was the size of a sheet of plywood, four feet wide by eight feet long. Paul built his own shelves, cabinets and countertops. He took pictures and developed them. He bought an enlarger, and the grade of his photography started to go from beginner to very good.

Paul was proud of that darkroom and the pictures that came out of it. He showed me how everything worked. Yes, he taught me photography. It was easy to get caught up with his enthusiasm. The results were so good. Photography became my hobby, too.

Paul joined the Army, too, and, after finishing his training, was sent to Hickam Field Airbase, Pearl Harbor, Hawaii. He was a photographer on that base. He wrote home often telling how much he liked his assignment.

Until December 7, 1941. Less than a year into his time in Hawaii, Paul was on duty as a photographer when Japanese aircraft suddenly attacked and strafed Hickam Field with machine-gun bullets. He was taking pictures. But he dropped his camera when he saw two men shot right in the middle of the airfield. He ran to them, picked one up, put his arm around the other, and started to carry and guide them toward a hangar and shelter. Bullets were whizzing past them as they crossed the field, but they made it. Paul was awarded a Silver Star medal for heroism. The only higher military honors are the Medal of Honor and the service crosses.

Another incident about my brothers is worth telling. When I was six and my mother asked me to do something, I tried to avoid doing it by whining, complaining and making it clear that I didn't want to do it. My brothers called me into the living room and told me, in no uncertain terms, "When Mom asks you to do something or to help her, you do it. We are a family and help each other. Got it?"

I got the message. I never said no to my mother again when she asked me to do something or to help her. After all, if my big brothers did it, I would do it, too. Isn't it interesting how a good habit can be learned and started at an early age?

I always looked up to my big brothers.

Left: The author's brother Paul with his Silver Star, awarded for bravery at Pearl Harbor. Right: The boys with their mother in the late 1920s.

CHAPTER 4

Our Family's Store

In 1928, one year before the stock market crash, my parents opened a Mom and Pop grocery store in our house. The U.S. economy was not going well. My mother and father would talk about it quietly, so that my brothers, John and Paul, and I wouldn't hear. Still, you couldn't help but feel that something overwhelming was starting to happen. Jobs were decreasing in number and availability. My father's job as a carpenter was now fewer days each week. Money was getting tighter. So my parents decided to try opening a store.

My father had many days without work, and he talked with his carpenter buddies. Two of them came over when they were not working, and with my father they eliminated our living room and a hallway, and relocated my parents' bedroom to a small addition in the back. Since we lived on a corner, they knocked out two walls, put in two large store windows and a large store entrance door. They added an "ice box" refrigerator, which used blocks of ice to refrigerate and preserve the milk, butter, meats, eggs and other perishables. The Mucha Grocery Store opened with its new shelves, counters and vegetable bins. We kids put the groceries on the shelves, loaded and dressed the windows. We had to be inventive every day, since none of us had any experience running a store.

Just four blocks away was the downtown Lebow's Super Market, where we often shopped for items we needed in our home but didn't carry in our store. Ours was the neighborhood store. It was small. We tried to carry what the neighborhood wanted to get in a hurry. We sold canned foods, cold cuts, soft drinks, milk and juice, vegetables and fruit, bread and rolls, candy and newspapers. People called it "the Mom and Pop Store."

We would open the store at 5:30 each morning and close it at 8 p.m. The neighbors came, wished us well, and bought some groceries. When someone opened the door and entered, a small clanging bell would ring, and we would hear it and come right out. If someone showed up before 5:30 a.m. or after 8 p.m., we would still open up to serve them. All you had to do was knock. Usually one of my parents would open the door with a cheerful "Good morning" or "Good evening," never saying, "We are closed now" or "Come back later."

I was seven when the store opened in 1928, and I was expected to total all the items that were purchased. So I would list each one and its price clearly, add them all up, then let the customer check. The first time I made a mistake in addition, the customer got upset. My parents also got upset. I quickly got good in math. I didn't make a mistake again. I double-checked the items and total before giving the book back to the customer to check. My brothers never had this problem, because they were nine and eleven years old.

Our cash register was an old-fashioned keyboard type that made a lot of noise when you pushed the keys to show the total. It summed the day's sales for our records as the amount of business we did that day. All receipts to customers were hand-written, including items, prices and totals. Customers always checked every item and the total. Nobody had a hand calculator in those days. The Depression had made us all "math smart."

We sold "penny candy grab bags," which came already packed in small brown paper bags. The bags were always the same size, but they didn't always have the same amount of candy inside. I would put them in the glass candy display counter, arranging them so the ones with more candy were on the bottom. Any mean kids (and there were a few) got the less-candy bags on the top. Everybody else got a more-candy bag from the bottom — especially my friends and all the little girls in the neighborhood. They sometimes got one free even if they didn't have a penny but did have a smile. I considered that "good merchandising," especially for me.

One of the breadmakers that supplied our store was Taystee Bread. They delivered bread about three times a week, with one of the deliveries giving us free "mini sample loaves." Even though small, they were still wrapped just like the full size loaves. I thought they looked "neat." (That was the expression in those days. "Cool" hadn't been born yet.) My mother loved to hand out a mini-loaf to a family as her way of saying "thank you" for coming to our store. And they would say "thank you" back. The neighborhood thought it was a special weekly treat in the Depression. "Thank you, Taystee Bread," we would say.

At age 10, I was allowed to operate the cold cut slicing machine. I cut myself only once. Once was enough to be forever careful.

We had six to eight neighbors who couldn't pay for their food until payday on Fridays. They would purchase during the week, then come later to pay "the book grocery bill." We would put their name in a three-inch-by-six-inch, 50-page notebook and list what they bought, item by item, and the price, and total it, and they would sign it. We would date each purchase and keep totaling it up until Friday, when they would pay up. The book would be used again and again as they needed it. Some families used the book a lot. After all, they couldn't use it in a larger supermarket. But at our place they could use it at 5:30 a.m. just to buy some milk or bread or cold cuts or fruit. Or even that penny "grab bag" of candy.

My parents never said no to anyone, even if someone didn't pay for weeks. They just didn't know how to say no to a family that asked for "book" credit. The times were that hard, and we could eat from the leftovers in the store.

In those difficult days, people just seemed to understand that we all had the same problems. Everybody would help each other, even if it meant sharing food with a family that was short of food that day. Many a mother would cook or bake something and give half of it to a neighbor, even if the giver's family was in short supply themselves. Ours was a closely knit neighborhood. The kids played together, and the parents struggled together.

Three blocks away was another neighborhood Mom and Pop grocery store. Each neighborhood bought from its own neighborhood shop, because they could walk over or send a child for the food items. It was closer, more convenient, and they were always treated like neighbors.

The Depression took its toll on the neighborhood families, but people stuck together and worked together to survive. In spite of all of the problems, you didn't hear many complaints after three years of the Depression. You were in it for the duration. You got tired of hearing about it, so you stopped talking about it. Others stopped and then they started trying to be a little more cheerful. That's when nobody wanted to hear the complaints anymore. We were all complained out!

We didn't know it at the time, but that was when the Depression was bottoming out, even though it still lasted for a long time. Gradually, we started looking toward the future. Things were picking up. It was a little brighter. The proportion of the good news in the newspapers was starting to increase. People were paying cash again for their food in our grocery store. My father, a carpenter, was working more days at his trade. We started to talk about the Depression as if it was a thing of the past, but never forgetting it. It was one miserable lesson.

The store stayed open for about six years. It helped our family a lot in getting through the Depression. But it closed when our neighbors went back to the local supermarkets with their cash payments. They didn't need our store anymore. We didn't have enough varieties of foods to fill their growing grocery lists. So my parents closed the store, and put back the living room, hall and bedroom as they were before.

To me, that was the end of an era. Jobs were becoming more available, and family life was getting back to normal. I was even allowed to end the weekly delivery routes of newspapers, magazines and movie theater handouts, which I had for about six years. I could concentrate on baseball, tennis, street hockey, school and studies, and being a full-time kid again.

The Depression was never an easy time. My family survived — somehow. We learned from it. Those lessons proved valuable later, in good times and in hard.

CHAPTER 5

Movie Dishes and 100 Fishes

The Depression wasn't depressing for me. As long as you're healthy and have friends and family, you can find something fun to do. We didn't have video games, computers or even TV, but we had good times.

The movies were a big deal during the Depression. *Frankenstein*, *King Kong* and *It Happened One Night* were huge hits in the early 1930s. Did you know that *Gone With the Wind*, which came out in 1939, is the biggest moneymaker of all time, when you adjust its box-office earnings for inflation? I delivered promotional leaflets for the Ritz in our town, so I never had to pay to get in. I went at least twice a week, especially to see the Saturday afternoon serials, like Flash Gordon adventures, cowboy movies and mysteries. The candies were less than a nickel, but I never could afford to buy them. I remember how you could not only get into the movies for 10 cents, but on Monday nights, each customer would also get a nice dish! They weren't cheap plastic. They were ceramic with colorful flower designs and glazed.

My mother and father loved to go to the movies together, and Dish Night was a natural. One time, a spooky film was playing and right in the middle of a tense, scary scene, the audience was dead silent, and my father's plate fell — probably on purpose — out of his hands. It hit the concrete floor with a resounding crash that made everyone in the theater laugh. Except my mother, who lost a plate. She didn't say a word until they were walking home after the show. Eight decades later, those heirloom dishes were still in use, at least on special family occasions, at the home of my oldest son, Peter, and his wife, Anne. It's a whole set — including big plates, dessert plates, soup bowls, serving bowls, a casserole dish with a lid, a sugar bowl, and a gravy boat. Except for one missing dish.

Right in the middle of the Depression, just one block from my home, a man built a miniature golf course on the lot next to his house. Hoping to make some money, he built wooden frames and used carpet for putting greens. For kids, it cost just a dime to play, and I loved it. There were ramps and curves, and even a windmill and a gorilla. The kids in the neighborhood got to be pretty good at miniature golf. But it was the Depression, and the course lasted only a couple of years. The fence started falling apart, weeds took over, and it eventually became a bumpy, grassy field. Later, a house was built there. But while it lasted, it was fun.

Often while walking home from Columbus Grammar School, I would see adults playing tennis, and it looked like another good game to play. The township courts were free, but where could we get a tennis racket? The balls were easy to get. When grownups played enough tennis, they would leave worn balls behind when they went home.

You should have seen us kids scramble to get an abandoned ball after we saw the players finish and go. When I got two balls, I was ready. Now all I needed was a decent racket. Six months before, I had picked up one that someone discarded because a couple of strings were broken. But I needed more strings.

Did you know that it's possible to replace the strings yourself? My brother Paul showed me how. See, rackets come with two long strings, one that goes back and forth for all the horizontal rows, another for the vertical ones. When a string broke, the proper repair was to replace the whole long string. But Paul's trick was to use the broken pieces people tossed away. So when a player at the courts would break one, I would ask for the old broken strings, and if they said yes, I pulled them out and took them home.

Paul took the time to show me how to tighten the existing strings on a racket, put in the not-so-new strings I just found, and knot them so they wouldn't come loose. Now my tennis racket was ready. I was eager to play. But I had no skill or experience. In other words, I was bad. All I could hit were home run balls over the tennis fence. Hitting a ball so that it actually landed on the court was a real problem. Playing was fun, but it wasn't tennis yet.

    Paul came to my rescue once again. He was one of the best tennis players in town, in my opinion. He could serve, smash, volley and backhand. He showed me how to grip the racket and make a level swing, so that the ball actually landed on the court. The age of miracles had just begun. Later, Paul showed me topspin and backhand, and that really got my attention. His best shot was his top-spin forehand. It was tough to defend against. I always enjoyed watching him play, but I could never beat him. Every game with him was a lesson to me. Besides, he was my instructor. A good one. And my brother.

    With two municipal tennis courts just six blocks away, it was easy for me to play with anyone who was willing. We could play for an hour, then we had to let someone else play, according to township rules. I would bring along a book to read when not playing. As soon as more kids showed up, we would play doubles. It was a great way to spend the summer. Every week, we got a little better.

    I soon got better at replacing broken tennis strings. I even started a little restringing business! I bought a new set of restring-your-own-racket tennis strings for twenty-nine cents, with money saved from newspapers and magazines I delivered and collected payments for. Then I charged players three cents (the price of a newspaper) to replace a broken string with a leftover, previously used one. It was a nickel if I put in a new string. This let me get enough money to buy a new set of tennis balls for fifteen cents. How I treasured them. I wouldn't use them for practice, only for play. Playing tennis made each summer better, and the practice helped me get ready for the high school team. But that lasted only one year. Then the school canceled tennis.

    I was still able to play and did. It was an interesting sport and I loved it. I taught it to my kids, and they loved it, too, but not as much as I did.

CARTERET HIGH SCHOOL

Stephen Mucha

CLASS OF JUNE 1939

Good times playing tennis even led to my second marriage (as you'll see in a later chapter, "A Few Tips About Marriage"). Tennis was a great activity that lasted for me until I was 79 years old, when arthritis stopped me.

My father loved to go fishing. Sometimes he would go alone, but most of the time he would at least take us boys along, because we liked to go fishing, too. Sometimes, the whole family would go. Sometimes, we would catch only a few fish. Sometimes, none. Once in a while we would catch a bunch, like four to eight fish, and we would feel happy that we had a good day fishing. We all loved to eat fresh fish, because my mother cooked them so wonderfully, lightly breading the fillets and frying them in butter.

Our family fishing gear consisted of plain bamboo stick poles with string, and a tackle box with hooks, lines, sinkers and a knife. It was all kept in an old large galvanized tub with side handles. That way, my father could just grab the tub and carry the fishing gear in one trip to the car. Whenever my father said,

"Let's go fishing!" you never saw us three boys move so fast to load the car. We would usually go fishing in the river at Sewaren or in Raritan Bay at Morgan, New Jersey. Someone, though, would have to stay behind to run the store.

On one particular day, my father took my brothers and me fishing. It was in the bay at Morgan. The fish were really biting when we got there. The porgies were running and we fished for hours because we were catching fish after fish after fish. At one time, we actually were catching a fish a minute. It was marvelous. I never saw fishing so quick and easy and rewarding. We didn't stop fishing until our washtub and extra bucket and burlap bag were all filled with porgies. We caught over a hundred fish. There were so many that we filled up the car. We were singing and laughing all the way home. We kept saying, "Wait until Mom sees all these fish that we caught!"

When we got home, my father planned for all four of us to march in triumphantly with all the fish at once to surprise Mom with the size of the catch. She was astonished to see over one hundred fish, all caught in one day, spread all over her kitchen floor.

My mother looked at my father and exclaimed, "I never saw so many fish in all my life! What are we going to do with all these fish?"

They looked at each other for a moment and started to smile. I knew something was going on, but I didn't know what. I kept saying "What? What? What?"

They said, "We are going to share them. With our neighbors, with our relatives, and with our friends." And that is what my parents did. They shared the fish. That was more important to them than putting them in our large "store refrigerator" to save for our use only. Or to sell them as "fresh fish" for the money it would bring. We boys were kept busy delivering packages of paper-wrapped fish. It was a wonderful day. I'll never forget it. Thank you, Lord.

Now, porgies weren't big, but they were delicious when my mother pan-fried them. Often, after a good time of fishing, my father would light up his pipe and recite the children's fish poem he learned as a little boy in Czechoslovakia. The English version goes like this:

*Little fishes in a brook,
Papa catches them on a hook,
Mama fries them in a pan,
Baby eats them like a man.*

I loved that little poem. Even today, I love to tell it to little children. I haven't found anyone who didn't like it. And that includes grownups.

PART 2

MONEY LESSONS FOR TODAY

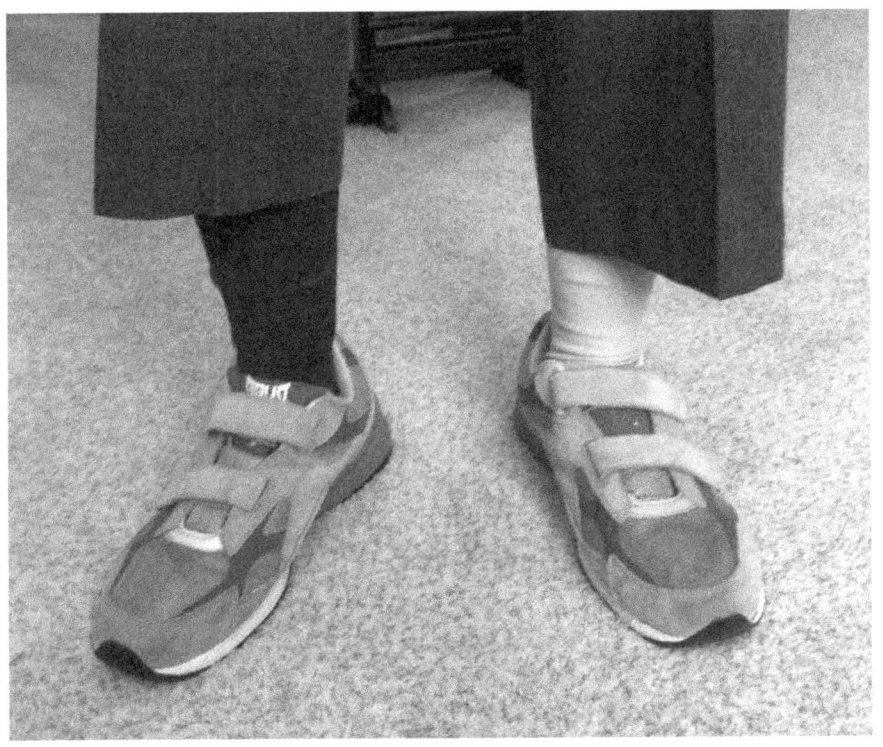

The author sports a pair of "Recession Socks."
His making the most of a situation caused some kids to smile.

CHAPTER 6

Hard Knocks and Recession Socks

In tough times, the government can only help so much. We also have to help ourselves, and each other. Just trying to cheer people up is helpful, too.

During the recent big recession, the tough times reminded me of how critical the problems were in the Great Depression. Then, when people lost their jobs, they looked for work, and, like today, too many had no luck. So, they often resorted to selling apples on the street. They had to do it to bring some money home to their families. I can remember seeing this, plus reading the apple stories in the newspapers, which cost three cents back then.

Nowadays, people are also working hard to survive uncertain times. Take this story about a man who lost his job and couldn't find another, so he started his own job as a handyman. Kevin called on us, and we gave him some repair jobs that I couldn't do anymore. After all, when you are in your upper eighties, there is a slipping decline in ability. After about a year of his help, Kevin said that we needed to have the gutters cleaned again. But this time, because they were dripping, they needed to be painted and waterproofed. It was January, and I worried that the paint wouldn't stick right in the cold. He answered, "I have painted gutters before at 40 degrees, and it worked out fine." With snow in the forecast, I knew he wouldn't be able to work for two days. But he was anxious to get started as soon as he could, and did the work for $200. He completed the job easily.

Next, he noticed that my garbage disposal was jammed, and fixed it in minutes. He might have saved me hundreds of dollars in replacement costs, but he didn't charge me for it.

Another time, our handyman said our roof shingles were getting old and moldy. He didn't do roofing jobs, but he recommended getting the shingles replaced. The job, he estimated, could cost at least $7,000 for our small ranch home. I thought about it and decided, "Not this year."

But a few days later, I thought about the recession, and maybe a roofer needed a job, even for a small house like ours. I phoned a roofer who was a friend and got a quote. It was $6,000. I didn't phone another roofer. I didn't get another price. I gave him the job. He did it about ten days later. He cleared off our old roof and put on a new one the very same day. Two days later, he came over to be paid, and he didn't ask for a penny more. "The weather was nice and warm for a November day, and the job went off without any problems," he explained. I'm glad I didn't get a second quote. These are tough times for many of us. I can't recall getting a break like that during prosperous times.

Now here's a more light-hearted story, about lifting people's spirits, even if was kind of by accident. My wife, Carol, and I had been giving a Children's Message in our Saint Paul Methodist Church in Willingboro, New Jersey, once or twice a year. The minister would give us the scriptures and the title of his sermon. And we would call all the children sitting in the church to come forward and we would deliver a short Children's Message to them.

But this time, Carol was visiting her son and his family in Alaska, when I got a call reminding us it was our turn to do the Children's Message. That Sunday morning, I went to my sock drawer to get a fresh pair of socks. But there wasn't a pair left. There were four socks, but each was a different color. I picked the two neatest colors, a yellow and a pale blue, and put them on, and went to church.

As I called the children to come forward to hear the Children's Message, a bright and observant little girl started to giggle. I asked her why. She pointed to my socks and exclaimed, "Mismatch!" I had no choice but to pull up my pant legs a few inches for all to see. The kids and the congregation burst into laughter. In defense, I muttered, "I needed a pair of socks this morning, and I went and opened the sock drawer. All that was left were four different color socks. I picked these two, and I call them my 'Recession Socks,' because they were all that were left. And that's what is happening to us in this recession. We are starting to run short, and having to take what is left."

When I delivered the Children's Message that day, I gave each child a plastic clip with these words on it: "Here's a clip to help you hold onto those things that you need in this Recession."

The kids were great, and I thought I did a pretty good job. But most of the comments that came after the service were about my Recession Socks.

People smiled and laughed. It just shows you don't need money to spread a little happiness. Since then, I have gotten into the habit of wearing my Recession Socks more often. And the people in church often greet me with, "What socks are you wearing today?"

CHAPTER 7

Popcorn and a Soda Retirement Plan

We took our grandson to the movies, and he wanted popcorn and a soda. The popcorn size he wanted cost $6 and the soda also was $6. So as grandparents we said no to the soda — too much money. But we bought him the popcorn. It was a good movie, and we enjoyed it. After the show, we picked up the popcorn bag and said, "You have one-third left, so take it home and eat it later." When we got home and were getting out of the car, we noticed that he didn't have the popcorn bag and asked him, "Where's the popcorn?"

"I threw it in the theater trash," he said.

My wife, Carol, and I asked, "You threw it away? That one-third bag of popcorn? Why?"

He replied, "I always throw it away. I don't want to save it for later!"

Now, that's the concept that lots of modern children and adults have — buy too much and throw some of it away, saying, "I don't want to save it for later."

That attitude is the seed of many financial problems, especially not saving for retirement. This philosophy thinks, "It's only a third of a bag of popcorn — what's the Big Deal?" But as it happens, it can be a Big Deal. Yes, it really can be a Big Deal. As I mentioned earlier, by saving a little here and there, my mother managed to bring six family members to America from Czechoslovakia over about eight years. Just as pennies and nickels added up then, quarters and dollars can add up today. To those grateful people, it was a Big Deal.

The philosophies of parents often differ from those of their children and grandchildren. "You are old-fashioned," say a lot of modern children and grandchildren. "You are spending too much," say the parents and grandparents.

Yes, two different philosophies.

Currently, on my credit card bill, the interest is two percent per month, which is twenty-four percent per year. Paying that much interest is crazy! Rates on car loans, mortgages and home-equity loans are much lower, though I am not advising you to take on those loans instead. Do all you can to pay off all your credit card balances each and every month.

Suppose you went on a trip to Hawaii, and you charged $2,000 on your credit card. Say your minimum payment was four percent, or $80 the first month. Half of that would be just for interest. If you paid the minimum every month, know how long it would take you to pay off your stay in Honolulu? Nearly ten years! In all, you would wind up paying $3,775 for your trip, including $1,775 just for interest. And that's just one expense. Over those ten years, many more purchases could go on that card, driving you deeper and deeper into debt. No wonder charge cards drive some people into bankruptcy.

So, when the credit card company offers you an "easy and small" minimum payment plan, who's really getting a good deal? The credit card company, at your expense.

I recently saw on television an announcement about a new set of computer games expected to sell about $6 billion worth. That's a lot of people spending a lot of money. Will you have to buy one and watch your debt balance go even higher?

Popcorn and soda can add up, too. Just follow along and see how. First, what could have happened if this were you and you had bought your child the cheaper $4 bag of popcorn and put the $2 you saved into your retirement fund, earning 4 percent interest? Also add the $6 for the soda you didn't buy. You may be surprised by what happens.

Is this your first lesson in cumulative or compound interest? Each year, interest adds to the total, so you start earning interest on the interest, then interest on the interest on the interest, and so on, while you still earn interest on the original investment.

To see how it can work for you, just look at Table 1A below. When the growth gets to Galloping Interest — where the earnings get bigger than the original investment — you are starting to be way ahead.

TABLE 1A
Retirement fund growth at 4% interest

Investment	After 10 years	20 years	30 years	40 years	50 years
$2	$2.96	$4.38	$6.49	$9.60	$14.21
$6	$8.88	$13.15	$19.46	$28.81	$42.64
$100	$148	$219	$324	$480	$711
$1,000	$1,480	$2,191	$3,243	$4,802	$7,107
Total growth	48%	119%	224%	380%	610%
Galloping Interest*		1G*	2G*	3G*	6G*

*How many times growth exceeds original investment.

That measly 4 percent turned into more than 600 percent growth over 50 years!

Now let's look at the power of regular saving itself. What if you spent a little less a week on food, beverages, lottery tickets, music, cigarettes, or your TV or phone bills, and saved that money instead?

Here's how it could add up:

TABLE 1B
Retirement fund growth just from regular savings

Savings	After 1 year	10 years	25 years	50 years
$2 one time	$2	$2	$2	$2
$2 per year	$2	$20	$50	$100
$2 per month	$24	$240	$600	$1,200
$2 per week	$104	$1,024	$2,600	$5,200
$6 per week	$312	$3,072	$7,800	$15,600

Wow, the price of one weekly soda or popcorn adds up to thousands of dollars! Makes you rethink the true, long-term cost of your spending habits, doesn't it?

Now, hold onto your hat, as we put the two together.

TABLE 1C
Fund growth with regular savings and 4% interest

Savings	After 1 year	10 years	25 years	50 years
$2 one time	$2.08	$2.96	$5.33	$14.21
$2 per month	$26.52	$296.35	$1,023.03	$3,744.92
$6 per month	$79.55	$889.06	$3,069.08	$11,234.76
$20 per month	$265.17	$2,963.52	$10,230.28	$37,449.21

Still think a popcorn and a soda (or a lottery ticket and a candy bar) can't add up to much?

Now, let's check out what happens with a slightly higher interest rate.

TABLE 1D
Fund growth with regular savings and 5% interest

Savings	After 1 year	10 years	25 years	50 years
$2 one time	$2.10	$3.26	$6.77	$22.93
$2 per month	$26.65	$311.98	$1,178.24	$5,161.41
$6 per month	$79.94	$935.95	$3,534.73	$15,484.24
$20 per month	$266.45	$3,119.84	$11,782.42	$51,614.14

On the $20 a month, that 1 percentage point difference turned into more than $14,000 extra over 50 years! Of course, because rates vary from year to year, and from one type of investment to another, you might do better than 5 percent, or have to settle for less than 4 percent. But these tables should encourage you to shop around for the best interest rate you can safely get. The difference can buy a lot of popcorn.

CHAPTER 8

Starting a Retirement Plan

One time, about 1991, I was standing in a line, when I overheard two men talking about how their retirement plans were working out, now that they were retired a year. One, a janitor at a school, said something like, "We never had much money. We had a modest home and an older car. We struggled through the years, raised children, and had little money left. But once we retired, we had three retirement checks every month. One from the Army, one from the state, and one from Social Security. We still have the same modest home that is paid for. But we just bought a new car, are traveling more, and are able to give some help to our children financially. And we have free medical insurance benefits for life. It was tough to save when the children were growing up. We don't need to now that we have three retirement incomes." Oh boy, was I listening. The story of the second man was similar.

Now, who was smarter? Me, with my college education and good jobs with companies that had no retirement plans (or requirements I didn't meet) and no medical benefits? The winner was the man with three retirement checks and medical benefits. He showed that planning for retirement doesn't begin after the children are grown. It begins with your first job. He was well-rewarded.

When I started my own business as a manufacturer's representative, the retirement plans were set up to be paid out of annual company earnings. Each person's IRA plan was individually owned, not company owned. It could be switched to another plan by the owner at any time. Years later, I retired with my IRA earnings plus Social Security. But my wife and I, about 1992, were still paying more than $4,000 a year for health insurance. Each. And today our medical costs are double that! Retirement is not cheap. It's a good thing our house was paid for.

We were still stretching our money more, especially with the economic troubles that picked up steam in 2008.

Will you be ready? Eventually, you will need a retirement plan. When is the right time to start? Is sooner better? How should it get started? What will it cost? How much is needed to retire on? Can you join an employer's plan? Questions, questions, questions! What you need are easy and helpful answers. How do you make a plan simple enough to understand and then make it work for you?

Fortunately, some simple plans are very workable. Here are two basic types to think about. Social Security really is not enough, and as people live longer, the government could face more problems keeping it funded.

The Company Plan. Many employers put money into a plan that pays ex-workers regularly after they retire. Sounds great. The hope is that the company's monthly check plus your Social Security check will be enough income. If you have your doubts, you can put some of your own paycheck into that plan, or into one of your own as well. Check the what-ifs. What if the company retirement fund always belongs to the company? They can use it as part of their assets in case the company is sold or gets in financial trouble. You probably read about companies doing this or going bankrupt, and their employees losing their health benefits and retirement income. If your company puts your retirement money in your name to control, or in the hands of some independent financial company, your retirement plan and income will be much safer because the company can't take it away. You may still lose those health benefits, though.

The Do-It-Yourself Plan. If your company doesn't have a retirement plan, you will have to save and invest your own money. It's not as cheap as Plan 1, but it can be a safe plan because the ownership is in your name, and you selected one or more financial or investment companies to work for you based upon their performance.

TABLE 2
One-Time Investment in Retirement Fund
Based on 5% interest

Investment	After 10 years	20 years	30 years	40 years	50 years
$1,000	$1,629	$2,653	$4,322	$7,040	$11,467
$3,000	$4,887	$7,960	$12,966	$21,120	$34,402
$5,000	$8,144	$13,266	$21,609	$35,200	$57,333
Total growth	63%	165%	332%	604%	1,046%
Galloping Interest*		1G*	3G*	6G*	10G*

How many times total growth exceeds original investment.

You have to start somewhere, so look at $1,000, $3,000 and $5,000 as a onetime investment in the first week of January, and what it can grow into. Or, if you want $2,000, just double the $1,000 column. For $4,000? Just add the $1,000 and $3,000 columns together, or use any combinations to get the total you plan to invest.

That was for just a onetime investment! Regular investing results in bigger payoffs. See the following table for adding a $1,000 investment each year for ten years, and then investing nothing more — just letting it grow to retirement age. This shows how important an early start is.

After all, you can't predict what will happen. You could lose your job, get sick, or have to pay for children's college educations, making it difficult or impossible to invest again for years. An early start could turn out to be the only chance you may get. Table 3 shows the results of investing once a year for ten years and then watching it grow.

TABLE 3
10 Years of Annual Investments in Retirement Fund
Based on 5 percent interest

Annual Investment	After 10 years	20 years	30 years	40 years	50 years
$1,000	$13,207	$21,512	$35,042	$57,080	$92,971
$3,000	$39,621	$64,538	$105,126	$171,240	$278,931
$5,000	$66,035	$107,564	$75,210	$285,399	$464,885
Total growth	32%	115%	250%	470%	829%
Galloping Interest		1G	2G	4G	8G

If you start to save at age 40, you can get 30 years of investment growth, about 250 percent, by the time you're 70. But if you start at the age of 30, this plan will Gallop an extra 220 percent (to 470 percent growth). So isn't it time you started planning ahead?

Of course, if you really plan ahead, like starting at age 20, your retirement plan will Gallop from 470 percent to 829 percent, and that is an extra growth of 359 percent in those extra 10 years. Can you get a better deal than an extra 359 percent? So think it over. Especially if you are in the habit of treating yourself to those costly goodies because "I deserve them and I want them now." How will this habit help you have money to pay your bills during your retirement?

Suppose you say that 50 years of working is too long, that you'd like to retire earlier, like at age 62. If you have ample money saved in your retirement fund, good for you. Do it. But what if, after you retire, you suddenly discover don't have enough savings? You may find yourself having to work again, but this time at lower pay, and saying to yourself, "Oops! That wasn't so smart." Working again is disappointing, even difficult, when you want to be retired. Your older body and mind may be less capable and slower. That is one reason you could be working for a lower wage.

Many people are still working at age 70 and even 75. I am one of those who started taking retirement income at age 70.5, mainly because I had to. There were too many financial penalties if I didn't. I actually kept working until age 75. So when the possibility of 50 years of interest comes up, don't just say to yourself, "Forget it. That's too long." Instead, think about how time helps interest grow. The first ten years of five percent interest growth is 62 percent, while the decade of growth between years 40 and 50 years is 442 percent, more than seven times as much. What a good reward that is for planning ahead and starting early.

By the way, if you would like to see calculations for more possible payoffs, go online and search for "compound interest calculator." Bankrate.com, for example, had a slew of helpful financial calculators, as of this writing.

CHAPTER 9

Thoughts About Investing

But where to invest? If I have persuaded you to save early and often, hurray! You got the message. Now I can't claim to be some financial guru, who knows the smartest way to help your money grow. You want the highest yearly growth you can get, but what's the best option? There are many choices: individual stocks and bonds, mutual funds, bank certificate of deposits, insurance annuities, and money market funds. You could even put your money into gold, real estate or collectibles, such as art. The potential payouts vary wildly, and so do the risks. So don't take my thoughts as gospel about investing! Far from it. For best results, you would wise to read at least several books by experts about the pros and cons of different investments, as well as to seek help from a trusted professional financial adviser.

I am just passing on some basic ideas that worked for me. I'm not telling you where to put your money. This is just a start in getting you familiar with some of the basic issues. You need to get your mind thinking about retirement now, to get those extra financial benefits down the road because of an earlier start.

As you look into different retirement plans, here are some questions you'll want answered:

1. What is the current rate of interest, or return on investment?
2. What has the plan paid over the years, especially the last two to three years?
3. What are the risks? Could money actually be lost?
4. How much is the starting or minimum investment? If the starting investment is more than you have, you can start a bank savings account and build it up to that amount.

5. Is there any incentive or bonus upfront, like extra percentage points of interest the first year or two?
6. Are there any fees?
7. What is the minimum yearly investment amount?
8. Are there any penalty charges for whatever reason?
9. Can you skip depositing a year or more without penalty? (You could have a bad year.)
10. What plan does the agent personally use?

Don't get burned like I did. When I started my own retirement plan, I was told to put it in a mutual fund selected by my insurance agent. I did it, and after four years of zero growth, I complained. He said to select a plan that pays a better interest rate. After checking a few, I selected one that paid, "up to 8 percent." So, I rolled my money over and a year later, noticed that I was getting only 3 percent. "What's going on?" I asked. The representative said, "We hoped it might pay up to 8 percent, but it's only paying 3 percent this year." I asked, "What did it pay the year before, and the year before that?" His reply was "3 percent and 3 percent."

I was puzzled. I went back to my insurance agent and complained again. He explained retirement companies run things their own way, and some are more successful than others. I finally asked the $64,000 question: "What retirement plan is your money in?" He told me. I asked, "What interest rate did it pay last year?" He replied, "7 percent." I was astounded. Here was a very satisfactory answer. And, it was right in front of me all the time. I just didn't ask the right questions.

Yes, I then rolled my retirement money over again. This time it was to the company my insurance agent had his money in. And it has paid very good interest rates over the years. For example, in the year 2002 when many money market funds were paying around 2 percent interest, my retirement plan paid around 5 percent. My wife, a retired school nurse, has three self-directed school retirement plans, all with different companies. Each paid approximately 5 percent for the years 2002 to 2006.

Many retirement plan companies may pay higher rates of interest. You have to ask the question, "What did it pay for the last three years?" instead of listening to the sales claim, "We can pay up to 8 percent." It pays to shop around, and do your research, especially when interest rates are low.

As for stocks, I just couldn't figure out a profitable technique for buying and selling them individually. So I tried getting help from a stockbroker. After seven years, there was still no gain. I was still at break-even in income. So I switched to another stockbroker. After ten more years, the results were the same. No gains. I couldn't figure out a successful system. Apparently, the two brokers couldn't either. Even during years when the Dow Jones Index was going up, the stocks that I bought went down. I just couldn't figure out why.

That's when I switched to mutual funds and decided to follow my own advice. They had mutual funds that were close to matching the Dow Jones Index. They often went up when the Dow Jones went up, and often went down when the Dow Jones went down. So, I tried to guess the trends by reading the business and stock columns and making my own decisions. I wasn't a professional at this, but the results were starting to get better. The Dow Jones went up for a while and so did my index funds. But I knew that another choice, money market funds, were steady in value. They were more like savings accounts, and they didn't lose money, even though the interest rate varied according to market conditions. So they were a good thing to have when the Dow Jones Index was going down. In the spring of 2007, when the market was getting tense and the future business reports were more negative, I switched my index funds to money market funds. They didn't pay much interest at that time, but they didn't decrease either. When the Dow Jones Index was going down a substantial amount, my previous index funds went down with it. I was in a safer place, being in the money market funds during that time.

I was only a small player with mutual funds. I found that mutual funds worked better for me with my selections over the last fifteen years, especially when compared to the previous years in the regular stock market. And the fees were less, too. In some cases, there were no fees.

The hardest thing of all is making a decision to switch, and when to do it. On that, I can't give any advice. Sometimes I guessed right. Sometimes I didn't.

You'll have to find an investment strategy that works for you. But I hope I have made my major points: Start early, and know how your investments perform, so you can make changes as needed.

Please keep in mind that many investments are risky, including stocks, real estate, and commodities like gold. Some years, they might earn high returns — better than any bank certificate of deposit — but you actually lose a lot of money in other years. What counts in the long run is the average rate of return. Say you put $1,000 in a stock fund, and it earns ten percent one year, then loses six percent the second year. It will have gone up to $1,100 then back down to $1,034 – a return of less than 2 percent compounded interest. The point is not to avoid stocks, just to be careful.

CHAPTER 10

Better Late Than Never

I didn't start my own retirement plan until I was about 47 years old. It was almost too late for me. Having four children made saving tough. But I had to start sometime, or I would be in for a rough retirement, trying to live on Social Security alone. If that didn't work, I might have to take a minimum-wage job because we old folks don't work fast enough to be paid more. And I didn't want to do that.

The only choice was to start putting money into my own retirement plan. It wasn't much, but I did get it started. After all, income from a partial plan is better than none at all.

Then an interesting thing happened. During the year, I would think about that little nest egg I started, and about adding to it at the end of the year. I would daydream about putting a little more in than last year. And sometimes I did. I didn't have to plan on getting started anymore. I was on my way. I would do calculations to project the current value to ages 70, 80 and 90. That perked up my interest a little more.

There was no steady plan of adding so many dollars per year. I put in money whenever I could. When I couldn't I didn't. But it was good that I started when I did. My wife and I watched the budget very carefully to try to make sure it would last if I was lucky enough to reach 78, which, at that time, was the average life span for a man.

By the time I was 70.5, I was ready (and required) to start withdrawing. I felt, though, that I just didn't have enough. Only about 40 percent of my savings was invested in my plan before age 60, and the rest was put in between the ages 61 and 70.5. I was sure I had started too late.

It turned out I was wrong. The more I looked into it, the better it started to look. The figures were a surprise. The interest dollars were more than I expected. The interest that kept on adding over those first twenty-three years showed that the investment plus interest totaled $189,602. Becoming excited, I knew that if I withdrew slightly less than I was getting in interest, the plan would not decrease that year. So I tried it, and it worked. For six more years, my retirement plan did not go below the starting $189,602.

As you know, inflation keeps costing more as time goes on. So I started withdrawing more in 1998. My average annual withdrawal over the first 17 years was $15,307 per year, and the total paid out was $260,216 until the end of 2008, the year I was 87 years old. There was still $100,198 left. Here it is in line table form, making it easier to visualize:

TABLE 4
My Retirement Plan's Growth and Payouts

What and When	Amount
Investment in 3 retirement plans from age 47 to age 70.5	$98,500
Total value of plans at age 70.5 (investment + growth to 1/1/1992)	$189,602
17 years of retirement income (paid out) until 12/31/2008	$260,216
Amount left on 12/31/2008	$100,198

I was surprised. I looked at the above figures and said to myself, "Hold on now! I put in $98,500 as an overall total investment over the years to Jan. 1, 1992. How come, after drawing seventeen years of retirement money, I still had $100,198 left at the end of 2008? Did the interest help that much for all that time?" The answer is yes, it did! It continues to add to the balance every month. It doesn't just stop because you are withdrawing some each month. You could say that for those first seventeen years of withdrawal, interest paid for the whole seventeen years and 100 percent of the $206,216 in retirement income.

Now, if you're good with a calculator, or with using Internet retirement calculators, you could quickly find out approximately how the numbers might work out for you. At least, you would have an idea of what could be available later. Be curious. Don't short-change yourself. Find out. It will be important to you when you do retire. Go to your bank or insurance company or financial adviser. You might be surprised at how much information you can get from them, or in any packaged arrangement you may consider.

Now, mind you, I didn't figure out this plan in advance. I just put in money when I was able, and later withdrew according to need. But I always knew that if I withdrew the same percent of money as the current interest rate, the balance would stay the same for that year and even longer. That's right, you would be living on the interest alone, as it built back up each month. When I started taking out over seven percent instead, my balance started to reduce faster than I wanted. But it was necessary, and it worked out fine.

Of course, having a wife who was good at making the checkbook balance every month helped a lot. It was good to have us as a team where we agreed on ways to spend. You just won't believe how many arguments it avoided.

Social Security helped a lot. Thank you, U.S. government.

So did my wife, Carol, having her own retirement plan in the works. She is younger than I am, and didn't start collecting till about a decade after I did.

CHAPTER 11

Mortgage Management

You bought a house, and go to your bank for a mortgage. The first thing that you tell them is that you want the lowest monthly payment possible, so the bank runs off sheets for a 30-year fixed-rate plan. The bank could also offer an adjustable-rate mortgage, where the initial interest rate is low, but could rise later, depending on market conditions. Many people simply choose one of these options without considering other possibilities. Unfortunately, paying off the house slowly can lead to problems.

As you know, my philosophy is to keeping putting money aside, any way you can, so you're better off in the long run. With a house, you build your wealth by putting money into owning it, not paying lots of interest. If you slowly pay off a house, years later you might be surprised how little you really own and how much is still due. The lender will have benefited more than you. You might have difficulty affording a bigger, better house, say if your family grows.

So I recommend a couple of ways to pay off the principle faster. One is simply to consider a shorter fixed-rate mortgage. It is easy for the bank to run off a copy of a 20-year mortgage plan or even a 15-year plan. The reason for asking for two extra plans, and their cost to you, is to see how much faster you will be paying off the principle, thus owning more of the house yourself, while reducing the amount of monthly interest. You'll be amazed! The long-term savings is a big pile of money with the 20-year plan, and an even bigger pile with the 15-year plan. It pays off the house in half the time, at a much lower final cost to you.

What if you can't afford the higher payments in the beginning? The second strategy might be best for you. Because of the cost of the house, and all sorts of other expenses, such as moving and new furniture, many people still choose the minimum payment plan, the 30-year mortgage. Before you pick one, be sure to ask if you can pay extra any month, or even make additional payments, without any penalties. If the answer is yes, you can, when you're ready, shorten the loan yourself. The extra money would bring down the principle, which means the interest on the principle would drop a bit. In turn, less interest means more of each regular payment would go toward the principle. The more you pay early, the more the benefit snowballs, and your equity, or ownership, builds.

It doesn't take a genius to make this plan work. Just try using it for a one-year trial period of paying off a modest amount extra each month, such as $50 or $100, and you will be well on your way to finding out if you like having the mortgage balance go down faster and the number total payments get reduced. Your credit rating should go up, too, because you paid your mortgage off faster.

Also, if you had a bad month and couldn't pay the extra, there wouldn't be a penalty or even a complaint from the bank. That's what my wife and I did. We signed up for a longer mortgage but paid it off faster. So be sure to check on all your options before you sign your mortgage agreement. It can save you money and grief.

CHAPTER 12

Career Advice: Earning and Learning

Some jobs, unfortunately, lead to nowhere. Many jobs offer nice working conditions — perhaps you can select your own schedule — and the work might not be difficult or demanding. But if a job pays little and fails to provide those important benefits, your life can be tough, both now and especially later.

You go to work because you needed the job, it was available at the time, and it's convenient. You live in the hope that in a year or two, a promotion or a change in your job rating or classification will bring you better pay and some benefits. But it may not happen. You feel stuck with the original job offer. That's when you find that you are in "a job that leads to nowhere." Usually, these jobs don't pay well enough for you to afford medical and retirement benefits anyway.

A friend of mine liked her retail job and the medical benefits it included. After many years, she was called in and told that her work time would be reduced by one hour per week, that she was being reclassified as part-time, and that her medical benefits would be eliminated. Are you shocked? It does happen.

Another friend disliked her job. The working conditions were unpleasant, and she had to handle a lot of complaints. But she was getting medical and retirement benefits, so she learned how to live with the job and stuck with it over the years, along with others in the same office. And she is glad she did. It was a lot better than having a job that leads to nowhere, especially because she was able to retire with medical benefits and a pension. So try to be selective when you're looking for a job. It can be hard to change later.

Increase your education, and your pay will often increase. Many have done this to get better and higher paying jobs. It's a good goal at any age, and gives you hope for a better future. A college education often leads to a tougher job. But with your increased skills you can handle the demands better, which is one reason these jobs pay better. Just imagine what you could earn if you got even more education and worked hard enough to earn a doctorate. It's not easy. Again, you make sacrifices today to be on firmer ground later.

Not everyone, of course, can afford the time or money to get more degrees. Thank goodness, many jobs offer training and lots of chances to learn by doing. Such opportunities for career growth can be invaluable.

From 1949 to the mid 1950s, I was a mechanical engineer working for a company that sold printing presses and related graphic arts equipment. I was happy working in the engineering department, helping with new products. Then a vice president told me that I should get a broader view of the company's operations by working in another department for a while. He said that I needed to get into sales for a couple of years to get an understanding of sales and marketing. I agreed, and a short time later, I was transferred into sales and assigned the sales territory where I lived. What an adventure that turned out to be. I had no sales experience. I was a rookie salesman.

The company had 108 salesmen covering the United States. After four months of eager effort, I was still No. 108 in the amount of sales. My branch manager noticed that I was breaking all records in the number of sales calls per day. One day, I made 22 sales calls, but I wasn't selling much. I was still last in total sales. My branch sales buddies would kid me with comments like, "Steve makes a lot of sales calls, but doesn't sell much," and, "He's too busy making calls to tell people what he is selling."

So, my branch manager, who was wise and understanding, arranged for me to attend an afternoon seminar on sales techniques. I did. The speaker was Jack Lacy, and more than 100 trainees were there. He talked during lunch and three hours more. Everything he said made sense. It was bound to, since I didn't know anything about selling. I was an eager sponge. He gave each of us his book on his methods. I listened and absorbed. I read his book that same day. The next day, I went to work with a new and informed attitude. Two months later, a new sales year began, and when that selling year ended, I had gone from No. 108 to No. 2. The next year, I was No. 2 again. (I was never No. 1.) The following year, I was promoted to branch manager.

What made such a difference? I researched my presentation in a way that would better fit the facts. Believing in what you are saying and using facts makes holding a longer discussion easier. It took more thinking and planning, but it made sense to me, and it paid off.

I sold printing presses. That is, I was trying to sell printing presses, but I was getting creamed by two competitors who had come out with models that were newer, faster and quieter. Our presses were an older basic design that was slower and noisier. But they saved customers money in several ways. Not only did they cost less to buy, they were smaller, and were simpler and faster to get ready to print. The break-even point between our machine and others was around 2,500 to 3,000 sheets per job. But there were a great many jobs that were under 3,000 sheets. I concentrated on them, and our printing presses were able to be very competitive.

Before, I was selling without focusing on advantages. Now I knew I had some, and good ones, too. I was coming up with better answers than I had only a month before.

The biggest objection was noise. My competitors had a stream feeder that made their presses faster and quieter — they "hummed" as they printed — while they claimed ours went "clunk, clunk." What a challenge! Was there an answer?

I found one. I suggested customers change the thought from "clunk, clunk" to "click, click," adding, "When you hear our press going *click, click* in your print shop, you'll know they're in operation making money for you. And you can even hear it from your office."

Using this newly acquired and enthusiastic attitude, my sales started to go up and away from the dismal sales record that had belonged to me. I was glad to get off the bottom of the list.

That Sunday sales seminar was an afternoon that saved my job and changed my career. I stayed in technical sales from that day on. It turned out to be a good choice. Not bad for a boy who was voted "most studious," "most shy" and "most quiet" by his fellow students in the high school yearbook. If you put your mind to it, you can probably do it. Give it a try.

Years later, I was ready to change from working for a large company to working for myself, as a manufacturer's representative. I didn't change the type of job. It was still technical sales, but instead of being a salaried employee for one company, I was paid commissions by a variety of companies. I just started working for myself and running the whole business. It worked out for me.

It pays to keep learning any way you can. It helps your mind grow. Everything that you see, hear and sense are experiences that go automatically into your mind when they happen, and it makes your mind work very much like your own personal computer. As you put more data into it, it will have more capacity, and therefore will have more information available for you to use. It is always your own *personal learning data bank*, unlimited in size and capacity, for you to call on *instantly* so that you can use it whenever you choose or have the need to. And you don't have to worry about the name of the program — where it's located in your mind and how to find it — or whether you'll accidentally erase it, because it is always *instantly available* — with fantastic memory, for you to use whenever you choose. You can analyze and make more and better decisions fast. And yet, it is privately locked in your mind, not linked into the Internet where some hacker can tap into it and wreck it with a virus. You can build your personal learning data bank to be very large and safe.

It may actually seem easier to make a decision when you don't have much input information or data available. After all, there's not much to decide or decide from. But it doesn't really have much of a chance to be the right decision, because it's just not thorough enough. How many times have you made a decision and then later had to say, "Oops! If I had only known what I know now, I wouldn't have made that choice." We've all done it! And too many times to count.

So, as you gather more facts or data, your mind (personal learning data bank) has more in it to analyze, before it makes a decision. It may be tougher to do, to go out and learn the extra facts/data, but any decision based upon more information has a chance to be wiser. And, because you can clearly see more, that wiser decision can be made quicker, with less work.

Most people have very good minds, but often not enough facts/data in them to use for making better choices and decisions. They wind up doing the best they can, which is often not very good. This creates problems they will have to work on or eventually correct. Is this you?

Are you aware that the job you get can expand your knowledge, because of the way it encourages you to keep on using it? Also, the more education that you have, the more chances you will get to keep on increasing your facts/data capacity. People who have brilliant minds usually have a good education, where they learned to develop their minds from classroom work and extensive reading. But you won't find those encouragements if you have a minimum paying job and a short supply of facts/data in your personal learning data bank.

CHAPTER 13

Too Good to Be True

How many times have you been told that a deal sounds "too good to be true"? Sometimes, even the salespeople say this! Take the deal now or lose your chance forever, they'll say.

I've had many such deals offered and just about every time that I took one, I got a rude awakening. It turned out to cost us aggravation and money, sometimes without getting anything back.

One time, my wife, Carol, and I received a phone call for a vacation that was "too good to pass up," and the price was very low. So we paid in advance for our Great Vacation Deal. A few weeks later, we phoned to set up our vacation, and were told that those dates had been filled. The only dates left were ones we couldn't make, so we were told to try again later. We did, and the new dates weren't available either. We never did get that vacation, but they sure got our money. Another lesson learned the hard way. The salesperson said, "This vacation sounds too good to be true," and it was!

Once, we went to an expo and had a good time. As we left, they asked us to fill in a card for a chance at a free vacation. It implied (but didn't say) that one card would be drawn, and only one vacation for one couple would be awarded. A few weeks later, I got a phone call with the caller saying, "Congratulations. You are one of the three percent selected for this vacation package, a three-day cruise and four days at Disney World in Florida, including a hotel, for only $295. And if you act quickly, your wife can be included for only $295, the same rate." The fast-talking salesperson said, "This vacation deal to Disney World and a cruise was too good to be offered again," so we agreed. The next day, after thinking it over, we decided to cancel. I telephoned the East Coast phone number given to me, and got no answer. I

63

telephoned my credit card company who told me that the $596 had been transferred two hours after I placed the order, and it was too late to stop it. Besides, the money was sent to another address clear across the country.

I was told to write a detailed letter of what happened to the credit card company to start a dispute claim to try to get my money back. It was also suggested I phone the Better Business Bureau in that eastern state where the sales call came from. I did, and the agency told me that they knew about the company, that it had been in business less one year, and had many phone calls and complaints against it. Lucky for us, our credit card company got our money back. Thank you, credit card company.

We have been a lot more careful since then, and try not to listen to these fast-talking salespeople with their deals that are "too good to be true."

Recently, a door-to-door salesperson tried to sell us a replacement set of sliding double doors that were more energy-saving than our thirty-year-old ones, at a "one time, buy it now" price of $3,000 installed. Lucky thing that I asked my oldest son, Peter, who said go a local Home Depot and ask for the same size and type of door, which turned out to cost $1,600 installed.

We try to be more careful about letting someone make a sales pitch that is "too good to be true."

I have seen advertisements claiming that if you buy their product, you don't have to pay anything down now and you can start paying in a year or sometimes two. Seems too good to be true, and often it is. Watch out for the fine print. There could be penalties, such as higher interest rates.

Here's a sales pitch that recently caught us. We needed an item that we saw advertised in the newspaper by a local store, which was part of a national chain. We went there and selected it and were able to buy it, supposedly for no down payment and no interest or twelve months. We should have known it was "too good to be true." But the people in the store were so helpful and the item was a good choice, so we signed up for paying a year later at no interest.

Big mistake No. 1 was that we forgot about the date. Big mistake No. 2 was that we expected a bill to be mailed to us in advance. None ever came. Two months later, we got a phone call from their collection agency that our bill was overdue and that two late charges were owed, if we didn't pay all of the bill today. And no, they wouldn't accept our credit card. They even wanted our checking account number. While I was on the phone, my wife quickly phoned our accountant, who said, "No, they could withdraw whatever amount they wanted." So, we refused to pay any of the charges, saying we expected a bill and none came.

After a lot of arguing, they said to mail a bank-certified check within the next banking day, and they would accept the original balance with no late charges or interest. That's what we did, and we did get back a signed postcard that the letter with the bank check was received.

I never before bought anything with no payment due and no interest for a year or more. After this experience, I won't do it again.

PART 3

LIFE LESSONS FROM NINE DECADES

Author Steve Mucha and his wife, Carol Copper, perform frequently as the Musical Muses.

CHAPTER 14

A Few Tips About Marriage

I've been married twice, and the second time has lasted more than thirty years! Marriage isn't easy, and its lessons are sometimes hard to learn, but here is some of my best advice for having a happy and healthy relationship.

1. Find and Be Someone to Treasure

Have you ever met anyone you thought was kind, considerate, understanding, and just plain wonderful? Someone who helped other people instead of putting them down? Someone who was supportive instead of critical? It was easy to fall in love with that person, and you got married.

Perhaps only then did you find out that there were compatibility problems you didn't anticipate. You didn't like the same things. You didn't enjoy the same activities. One wanted to save for the future, and the other said the future is now — let's spend and enjoy it. Maybe one argued let's have children now, versus let's have children later.

Getting married is no guarantee that the other person will eventually agree with your views and desires. But many go still go ahead, telling themselves or others, "We'll work it out. You'll see!"

Then marriage starts becoming less fun, turning into more of a running argument and a chore. The one who is more controlling will probably say something like, "We're married now, and you've got to make the best of it."

Life is very different for the couple who, before marriage, checked into compatible interests to make sure they were a pretty good match. With such couples, fewer disagreements and arguments were ahead.

Wouldn't you like to have a marriage where twenty-five years later you still smiled at each other many times a day? Wouldn't it be a blessing to keep finding your partner in life was still wonderful and beautiful, like when you first got married? Don't trust to luck only! Help make it happen. Choosing a nice person is a good start. But it is not the only thing to rely on. Nice people have been getting divorced for years. That's one reason why approximately half of first marriages wind up in divorce.

Becoming a treasured mate doesn't just happen. It takes effort by both parties. Rarely does a marriage work out if only one person makes an effort while the other stays controlling and selfish. We all would like to have control and keep doing things our way. But do you really want to do that at the expense of the one you said you loved and promised to cherish?

You know what's a simple way to show love? Just try to be happy. Instead of complaining about your problems, and dragging the other person into frustrations that can't be helped, do your best to focus on the good things. Smiles say "I love you" better than frowns do.

2. Don't Compete With the One You Love

My wife, Carol, and I can't play tennis anymore due to arthritis and other age-related problems. Years ago, while we were both divorced from our first spouses and had started dating, I offered to teach her three teenage children how to play tennis. She brought along her own racket and we all played together on the same tennis court.

Since Carol was a beginner, she asked me to teach her. I told her that I wouldn't because I wanted to date her, and that tennis instruction includes a lot of criticism that might turn her off to her instructor.

It was one of the smartest moves I ever made. She told me that she was also dating another tennis player, named Frank, and that he would teach her. I repeated that I wouldn't, but I offered to pay for some lessons. So she took some instruction from Frank. In two weeks, that was the end of him.

A new tennis instructor was good, and so was her progress. Her tennis got better, and so did our dating.

At first, I would give Carol a handicap of two points. Since tennis scoring goes from Love for zero to 15, 30 and 40, we started each game with 30 for Carol. I won all the games. She didn't want me to ease up and let her win. She wanted to win on her own. The instructor was a big help. We played a lot, and it didn't take too long for her game to improve.

The handicap then changed when she started winning more than half of the sets we played. I still gave her two points when I served (she insisted on my not easing up when I served), and one when she served. And she just kept getting better. We started playing tie-breakers on those tough games, since in tennis you have win by two. A score of 40-40 is called "deuce," and then it's "ad," or "advantage," for whoever gets a point ahead.

As time went on, she got to one point only when I served. I recall that we played tie-breakers about a third of the time, and she would laugh and pump her racket when she won. We were playing competitively, and it started to be more fun and great exercise, too. We never got in the habit of getting into a long argument over a questionable play. It was as if we had an unspoken rule to take turns to be generous on a debatable decision.

When one of us won by a big score, never were any derogatory remarks made, like, "I creamed you today!" or "I am a better player than you," or "You play like that, and I will win every time." It's great to win. Everybody loves to win. If you want to play your opponent again and keep a friendship, don't rub it in. If you "rub it in," you may find yourself "rubbed out." Most people hate show-offs and poor sports. It won't make many friends for you. And it could threaten a friendship or dating relationship.

When Carol would win, often she would say, "I was hot today," and would grin and sometimes lean over and kiss me over the net. So I won, too!

After Carol took about six months of lessons, she and I were playing, when another couple suggested we share the court and play a set of doubles. We agreed and after five games, they were ahead five games to zero. They were good. Then a very interesting thing happened. Carol just started making a shot she had been working on for weeks. It suddenly came together. It was her first forehand smash from the backcourt. "Wow!" I said as she made that shot and won our point and game. She then made several more forehand smashes, and we actually recovered from losing the first five games to win the set at 7-5. She and her new shot made the difference that day.

We then joined a Parents Without Partners monthly tennis party night. After switching partners back and forth, they called for a couples challenge round, and we entered it. We won our first set, advanced, and won our second set. When we won our third set, we won the round. We were both surprised and elated. When the next month's tennis party came, we entered the challenge round again. And we won again. Again we were surprised and elated. For the next two years, we went undefeated, and that included our playing against a couple of two-man teams who paired up specifically to beat us. We felt pretty good about that. Nobody beat us in doubles play, not even teams with a man who had defeated me or a woman who had defeated Carol in singles play. Together we were better.

When we got married, we were no longer eligible to play in that tennis group. Our lives had changed, but we didn't stop playing tennis. We played for more than twenty years before aging and arthritis took its toll. Then we switched to music, which, once again, we did together.

3. Compliments Beat Criticism

It is easy to criticize, to say things like, "You are wrong!" or "You messed up!" or "It's your fault!" or any negative words meant to put someone down. You could then add, "I was just correcting you — trying to help you do it right!" But the meaning is clear: "You are wrong. Just do it my way, which is the right way, and don't argue with me!"

We've all done it. Sometimes we do it thoughtlessly, sometimes we just react, and sometimes we do it to control. But whatever the reason, the results wind up being selfish and harmful. When criticism is a habit, problems will escalate. I know because I have been there, and I don't recommend this way of talking to anyone.

In my second marriage, I did better. I can remember an incident in our first week. Carol had lost her car keys. She looked for ten minutes and said, "I am a klutz, losing my car keys and not finding them." My first thought was, "You said it, not me!" But somehow I bit my tongue and said nothing. I offered to help, and we both went looking. Ten minutes later, I gave up after looking everywhere. A half-hour later, I heard Carol yell, "Whoops, I found them!" She came into the room holding up the keys saying, "They were in my jacket pocket in the closet all the time." I quickly exclaimed, "Sherlock Holmes solves the case of the missing car keys!" We both laughed. At the moment, I didn't realize how good and positive were the words that I said, until she said again, "I am a klutz for forgetting where I put them."

"No, you are not," I said. "You are a Sherlock Holmes, and don't argue with me!" We both burst out in laughter. At that time, I still didn't realize how well I had responded by using "positive criticism" instead of negative. There were no hard feelings, because no negative remarks were made. It was then that I realized that I had made a positive criticism. I thought about it, liked the results, and gave myself an A+ for doing it.

From that day on, whenever Carol or I would lose our car keys — which was often — no harsh or negative words were ever said. I also have to admit that a lot of the time, Carol would find *my* lost car keys. Again, I would exclaim, "Sherlock Holmes strikes again!" That always got a smile from her.

Over the years, I tried to use positive criticism again and again because of the happier way that it always seemed to work out. I was learning to like it. Besides, Carol has now turned out to be the Sherlock Holmes in our family. Interesting isn't it, how a positive remark at the right time can have a good influence on a person's overall attitude, activity and happiness? Let me correct that. It has a good influence on both persons' attitudes, activity and happiness.

I don't have to tell you how negative criticism will tend to destroy or at least hurt a person's confidence. After all, negative criticism is aimed at stopping, shaking or destroying a person's ability to keep performing the way that they normally would.

Now let's talk about direct and indirect compliments. Some people have trouble making direct compliments like, "You did a good job!" or "That was a nice thing to say!" or — and this is a tough one — "You are right. I agree with you."

So often, complimentary words just don't seem to want to come out. They can be difficult to say. So you don't say anything or maybe make a half-hearted compliment like, "I guess it will work OK" or "You look all right" or "I don't see anything wrong with it." You might feel a bit foolish, because you know that a more positive comment would have been a lot better. You might feel a little funny inside because your remark just didn't come out right.

If you just won't make direct compliments, you could be a prime candidate for making indirect compliments. But don't do it in a negative way. Practice a little and start to learn to make clever indirect compliments, and you will probably like the results. So will the person who gets your compliments.

Here are a few winners:

I can't remember when you didn't look nice.
I couldn't do it as well as you did.
If you keep doings things that well, it could become a habit.

4. Be an Adaptable Idealist

One morning, at breakfast, I said to Carol that one of the things I loved about her in our "courting days" was her ability to deal with a sudden change in plans. Maybe there was a mix-up about the date or time, or maybe an event was postponed or cancelled for some reason, like the weather. She would say, "Let's check our options," and would concentrate on a switch in plans.

After a couple of times of seeing her switch to something just as good or even better, I began to marvel at her ability to re-aim our day to some other activity. And how it always seemed to turn out well.

This is what I call being an "Adaptable Idealist." Even if the new plan didn't work, it was still fun to see her work through our day together. One of our grandchildren, Kevin, recently said, "I like to do things with Grandma, because she is so adventurous." I agree!

Over the years, I have seen many Adaptable Idealists. I'm not talking about me, but about people who see the world as a good place to be, and who want to help it keep being a good place. I can appreciate seeing what they did and how they did it. It's been fun to watch. I have seen many mothers doing it with their children as they were growing up, by switching activities and plans and interests. Those children would then pass on this optimistic attitude to their families and others. Such creative determination keeps our country from going to pot. It is a very positive help in trying times, especially since some people don't give a damn about the Earth and its condition or future, just as long as they get their share of what they want now.

Among the Adaptable Idealists helping our world right now are doctors, nurses, philanthropists, scientists, inventors, teachers, their staffs and assistants, and everyday citizens, including senior citizens, who volunteer, volunteer, volunteer.

Many husbands have been happy to recognize their wives' growth and helpful influence at home and in the world. I am one of them.

CHAPTER 15

Second Chances and Second Best

Say you were on vacation, and you saw a snow-crested mountain peak. It was a wonderful scene. But you didn't pull out the camera just then. When you come back later, clouds have rolled in, and you can see only the bottom half of the mountain, but not the beautiful snow-crested peak. You missed a beautiful picture, because you assumed it would be there later. And it wasn't.

There are times each day that if you did it now instead of later, said it now instead of later, went to see it now instead of later, you could have made a difference in your life. You can't bring a special moment back to the way it was, at the time it was. Maybe it just wasn't convenient to do what you needed to do when it happened. I know it is often easier not to do it now. And even easier not to do it at all.

Don't let it wait. You don't want to say afterward, "If I only did this before, things would have been so different." Don't overlook the value of the small decisions made at the right time, compared with a big decision you are forced to make later.

If you get in the habit of making the moments count, you will find the rewards far greater than the empty benefits of stalling, avoiding or delaying — and regretting. I know this well, because over the years, I've made many of the empty-benefits choices. But I still keep trying to act on new opportunities.

Many people have become successful because they came up with a timely job or business idea and ran with it. They found a better future and better income. So, if you have an idea that works and can fill a gap in the system, whether it be a new product or a change in how to do something, consider it carefully. Filling a needed niche could be a chance to upgrade your life and your future along with it.

There are thousands of stories about people who took the idea route and found success. Many of these people presented their ideas to bosses. If the boss likes it, your reputation goes up, and so does your confidence. But many others were told no by their own company or other businesses. So these people started their own enterprises, leading to many success stories. That is what America is about. If you think you can, and you are prepared, maybe you should try.

I was a sales manager in a big company, and I kept seeing executives play the rough game of corporate politics. I didn't know how to play that game, nor did I want to. So, when my politically oriented boss became a loser in the game, I lost my job, too. The personnel manager said they had a sales manager's job for me in another area. I told him that I didn't want to play company politics, and I was thinking of getting out and starting my own business. He was very understanding and suggested that I phone in sick every Monday (which he would approve if anyone asked) and spend those Mondays trying to get started. I did, and two months later when our division closed down, I was in business. I became a manufacturer's representative. The first year was rough. The second year was profitable. I was started. And I never regretted the move, even though I worked longer hours than ever before and was faced with serious business decisions over the years.

Maybe you think you're just not qualified. Or not ready. Or don't have enough education. Or don't have enough start-up money or savings to live on. Maybe you tell yourself it's not your fault, there's nothing you can do.

Many people tell themselves these things, especially in difficult times. But don't get stuck on the complaining side. Try to move to the action side. Even if you are right, that you're not ready, don't give up. Try to climb the ladder one rung at a time. Write down your ideas. Talk to people, because maybe they can help, if only to make good suggestions. Any idea can then be made into a plan. No matter how small, it can be a goal to work for. Activity in finding a new direction will start you thinking positively. That's so important today, when negative thinking often seems to take over.

I have a friend who recently lost his job and the benefits that went with it. After checking in all directions for two months, he found another job. He was glad to get it, even though it was less money and had no benefits. Times were tough, and he had to take it. That start can help him get going.

We are all in the same fix. It's easy to blame Wall Street, banks and insurance companies for selfish activities that put millions of people in unfair financial positions. If you cry and complain, "It's not my doing" or "It's not my fault," you would be right. But talking and complaining won't get you out of the pit. Making a plan will start to accomplish something for you. Even a small plan is a good start, like the "Popcorn and a Soda Retirement Plan." The results can really add up over many years, not just in money but in your overall philosophy.

Perhaps you're afraid of failure. There's nothing wrong with failing, if you gain some valuable lessons! Now you know more than the next guy just starting out. Next time, you'll know better. Just step back and do some honest assessing before taking the next plunge.

A scientist tries an experiment. It fails. He tries again. It fails again. He makes changes and tries again and again and again. Sometimes there is success. Often there is failure. But does he quit? No. "I'll give it one more try," he says.

And that is what many millions of people have done over the years. They kept on trying until it worked better or solved the problem.

Life is like that. We couldn't count all the people who advanced because they kept on trying, maybe advancing from where they work to another company or another line of work, perhaps finally starting a business of their own.

And here's a comment on second marriages. If your first one has failed (and about half of them don't last), go into a second marriage with the idea that this time you'll do better. Be more understanding. Be less critical. Be more helpful. You can add some of your own thoughts here, too. The chances are your second marriage will work better. Mine did. And yes, I tried and did a lot of those above suggestions ... the second time. As a result, my second marriage is still working. Thank you, Lord, for a second chance.

Also, know you don't have to be the best at anything to have a good job or a good life.

I was never the best on my high school track team. I ran the half-mile and always came in behind Warren, who was our star half-miler and the county champion. One time, I broke the county half-mile record by 1.8 seconds, but Warren finished a tenth of a second ahead of me and I was second-best again. In three years of track, I never beat Warren, no matter how hard I trained and tried. He was always one step faster. He was the best and would get five points for winning the race. I often got three points for coming in second, and according to our track coach, those three points often helped our team. One time he said, "Warren's five points plus your three points made eight points and we won the track meet by two points — good job!"

We all want to be the best. We don't want to come in second. So, a lot of us just quit trying, reasoning, "If I can't be the best, then the heck with it! I quit!" Such thinking can start you sliding to a lower rung on the ladder of life.

But second best can be good, even great. No good team can exist without a lot of second-best players. In a school, a principal is selected because that person is supposedly the best. But could a school exist without its teachers? Don't even try to run a school without that big and important staff of teachers. It just isn't possible. Besides, one principal couldn't do his or her own job plus the work of even one or two more teachers. Not even in a twenty-four-hour day. Say that a hospital has the best director, and some of the doctors are the best at their own specialties. Could they add on all those duties performed by nurses and other assistants? Not possible! So, look at your job and the way that you fill it. Wouldn't there be a gap if you weren't there performing your duties?

In the larger scheme of things, being second best is great! Wouldn't you like to be the second richest person in the world? Or the second happiest? Or even in the Top Ten? We all need to learn to be happy and satisfied with doing our best, and not worrying too much about comparing ourselves to others. So, don't give up just because you are not the best. Look at your own accomplishments with pride. There will still be times when someone in your family, or friends in a group activity, will look up to you and say you are the best.

CHAPTER 16

A Better Cup of Coffee

Ah! That morning cup. It helps wake you up, and it has a nice habit-forming flavor. I've had my morning cup of coffee for many, many years now, and still look forward to it each day. I want to watch the sports summary in the early morning, usually around 6:30 a.m., so I feed the cats first. They just won't tolerate waiting. They will follow me around and let me know with continuous meows that they come first, that I need to feed them now. What choice do I have? So I do. Then I am allowed to make that pot of morning coffee. While it is in the making, I put the TV on to tape the sports summary, and then get dressed and fix some whole wheat toast. I switched from white bread when I retired, because my wife said whole wheat is better for me, and the doctor agreed. What choice do I have? Even the cats watch over me.

Then I put on the margarine and marmalade or jam. When I do get to sit down to the sports replay, I am ready to say "Mmmm" with my first taste of morning coffee and toast.

I have been doing this for many years, but now with extra enjoyment. This is the story of how I found a better cup of coffee about 2001. We were on vacation in Germany, visiting Carol's son Steven and his wife, Monika, and her parents. Monika's mother took us to see the German folk festival Fasnacht, which started at 5 a.m. It was still dark, but once the celebrating started, all the lights went on, and the music played all day as the many bands marched through the city streets. It was a wild and wonderful and beautiful musical and family day.

Then we went on to visit my granddaughter Corinne, an art student studying that year in Rome. The very first morning, she took us to a sidewalk cafe for a cup of coffee. It was cappuccino. It had good coffee flavor with a frothy foam layer of milk on top.

We took one sip, and couldn't say anything but, "Ahhh!" It was that good. We went there every morning for the five days we stayed. We bought the same coffee and said "Ahhh!" every time.

When we got back home, there was no "Ahhh!" after sipping my home-ground coffee. I thought about buying a milk frothy foam machine. But the machine was designed for restaurant use, and I couldn't see paying the hundreds of dollars to have it just for my morning coffee. So I didn't.

The flatness of my cup of morning coffee continued, but experiments began. I wanted that good Italian taste. I warmed up milk and poured it on top of the coffee, but it just dissolved into the coffee. Oops Number 1. The next day, I warmed up the milk and whipped it with a whisk. Same result. Oops Number 2. After trying more combinations, all I got was Oops Numbers 3, 4, 5, 6, et cetera.

So I tried a new direction. Using a normal coffee teaspoon, I added two heaping teaspoons (not two scoops) of vanilla ice cream into the already made cup of coffee, and then microwaved it for another 30 seconds or so. That was it! Success! The frothy foam was there. A white milky coating lay on top of the coffee that looked great and made the coffee taste even better. Yes, I've tried strawberry and butter pecan and even chocolate ice cream. But vanilla is the best, for my taste.

That's what makes my morning cup of coffee taste better. Every day! I just thought you'd like to know how it came about. And stayed. In its own small way, this story shows how a little experimental effort can create a success that lasts for years. Who knows? I don't see how I could sell my idea, but maybe yours could turn into a living.

CHAPTER 17

My Great Golf Idea

Golf is a wonderful game. You get a healthy long walk of at least three miles (if you don't take a cart), and a lot more if you spray your shots to the right or to the left. Golf is a happy time with friends, plus a lot of good fresh air and Vitamin D. Even my doctor said playing was good for me. It also passed on some long-term benefits for my later years.

For years, I played for fun and recreation. I was lucky enough to have found three nice guys to share this weekend golf with. We would play as teams, with partners rotating every month. We kept team records for wins and losses for the whole year, as well as individual averages on putts and wins. Handicaps did have a way of keeping things close, so it was often close enough that we would be playing at the end of December to still determine who won what. (Yes, we even played when the ground was frozen. The ball bounces farther and even hops across the frozen lakes!) It was playing for fun, exercise and friendship, with a minimum of money passing in and out of pockets. We bet just enough to make it interesting — like fifty cents for the best score on the front nine holes, fifty cents for the back nine holes, and fifty cents for the winning team, plus a dime for greenies and birdies. Greenies are for hitting the green in the fewest shots, with closest to the hole breaking any ties. Rarely did someone lose more than a dollar.

We had many interesting experiences. One time, one of our players named Les hit a great fairway wood shot, and the ball rolled on to the green, about ten feet away from the pin. We were applauding his shot while walking to the green, when a dog suddenly ran and grabbed the ball in his mouth and ran away with it into the nearby woods. Les ran after him, yelling, "Put it back! Put it back!" We found the ball in the woods. The dog was friendly, but wouldn't listen to anyone. Poor Les kept pleading, "Pick it up! Pick it up!" In the end, he had to play the ball where it lay. He wasn't too happy the rest of the day.

One windy winter day, Les had another great three- wood shot, where the ball landed short of the green, bounced onto the green and ran fifteen feet uphill past the pin, leaving him with a downhill putt. As he walked up to the ball, a gust of wind moved the ball a bit back down toward the hole. Les said to the ball, "Go! Go!" and kept yelling encouragement as the ball kept moving very slowly toward the pin. The rest of us were frozen in motion, watching that golf ball slowly head right for the hole and then actually drop in! Les let out the biggest yell. It was, "Eagle! Eagle!" When the rest of us finally came back to our senses, we realized that Les actually had an eagle two on a par-four hole. What a fantastic shot. Even if the wind helped a bit. As we walked back to our cars, Les kidded us by saying, "I played it that way!" You can see why I loved those guys. They were great, and the games were a lot of fun. I was lucky enough to play until I was 79, when arthritis stopped me.

You're not as sold on golf? Your experiences weren't so positive? So what's the problem? The game is tough to learn? It's frustrating trying to shoot some holes in par? It's exasperating when you have a bad lie? Infuriating when you get a "fat hit," with the ball not going far ... and crooked? But that happens to all golfers, occasionally to experienced ones, more often to the rest.

You don't have to be good at golf to have a good time. But you do need to know a couple of obvious things. And I have a tip that can make a big difference, and make playing a lot more fun. It's one more example of how anybody can have a great idea. It even turned into my first book, *How to Break 100*, which my son, Peter, helped me write and get published in 1982.

I was a hacker, getting a lot of bad hits and scoring too high. My best rounds were over 100 — dozens of shots over par. All I wanted was to play better and not be embarrassed. Was it possible to play just an enjoyable game, with a medium score that included some good shots? I wasn't asking for the impossible, like playing a mixture of pars and bogeys. I just didn't want to practice often or take a bunch of lessons that would exceed the family budget. So I struggled with my high scores and exasperating play for more than fifteen years. That is, until ...

One day, while we were on a family vacation, I went to play golf. As I warmed up with some practice swings on the first tee, I noticed something I had overlooked before. I was warming up on the first tee, swinging a golf club, clipping the grass. But the club wasn't clipping the grass even with my left heel, the place where I thought all shots should be played. I wondered why. I swung again. Again the club was clipping about six inches closer to the center of my stance. I wondered, "What would happen if I played the ball there?"

After we teed off, my ball was in the fairway. Then I took that practice "Check It Swing," and again noticed the grass was clipped approximately six inches closer to the center of my stance. I decided to play the ball in that position. Much to my surprise, using a five wood, I got a straight and solid hit. My opponent's ball was near the same lie, and he got a fat hit, hitting the ground first and squirting the ball a short distance to the right. He muttered a few popular golf words. As we walked along, I wondered, "Should I take a Check It Swing each time?" I did. It worked again and again. That was the day my golf game started to wake up — all because I found an easy way to correct for downhill and uphill lies.

It got me to thinking, "Is there another easy-to-learn technique that could help me play better?" I found two more and I shot my first 88! That was about twenty strokes better than I was previously scoring. One easy idea that helped was to proportion my backswing for changes in putting distance. I used an eight-inch backswing with an eight-inch follow-through to stroke a ten-foot putt. A twelve-inch backswing and follow through worked for a twenty-foot putt, and sixteen inches worked for a thirty-footer, and so on. Don't wrist-putt with this technique. Keep the wrists firm. That's what makes the proportioning backswing work.

The third easy-to-learn technique is proportioning the backswing for those shorter chip shots to the green. Again, without any wrist action, make the backswing and follow-through equal length. Avoid body turn as well, because it will generate extra power. You will have to determine how much swing to use by trial and error. But be sure that you do a test "Check It Swing" to see where to play the ball so that you don't get a fat hit.

These were the three easy-to-learn techniques that took my average score down from 108 to 88. After a few months, my average actually improved a couple of more strokes, as I got better in executing these swings.

Now for some comments about golf clubs. I wanted those new graphite-shaft clubs. The first time one of our group showed up with one, he boomed his tee shot 250 yards. That was about sixty yards farther than my usual tee shots went. Yes, I was impressed. Then the shaft broke on the back nine. That made me think, "I better wait a year or two, until the clubs get better, or the price drops a lot."

A couple of years later, one of our foursome was sick, and we invited a friend to join us, since his group was away. He was very excited to play with his new and expensive full set of graphite-shaft clubs. His tee shot went 250 yards right down the middle. He had a big swing. He said, "Big swing delivers big hits." His big swing also put about half of his tee shots in some awkward locations, like the trees. An extra stroke was needed to get back in the fairway.

I shot a 90 and he shot 102, above his average. "New clubs take a while," he said. That made me think, "I better not spend a lot of money on those new expensive clubs." I couldn't anyway. My budget couldn't handle it. I stayed with clubs from the $10 to $20 bargain barrel at the store. Some were bad, some turned out great. I thought I made out better than my friend who paid $2,500 for a complete set of new graphite shaft clubs, only to replace them a year later. When I found a club that worked, I stayed with it. I didn't need great clubs. I wasn't a great player. One year, only one, did I average 82. I even shot par for 18 holes one day in a golf league on a shorter course. Playing golf for enjoyment and exercise was my aim. Succeeding on a low budget made it extra satisfying.

CHAPTER 18

I Remember My Children

Author Steve Mucha in December 1958 with his four children (from left): David, Peter, Janet and James.

My first wife, Shirley, and I were lucky enough to have four healthy children. I still remember some of their exploits as they were growing up. Some events made me shudder and some made me laugh. But overall I have wonderful fond memories of their activities. So I have selected a fond memory of each to tell you about. I'll do it chronologically so there are no family arguments.

Janet

Janet, born in 1949, was a pretty and vivacious girl, who could also be a handful. With her brothers, she loved being helpful and guiding. I can remember one day calling for the children, and there was no answer. So I went looking for them, and finally found them sitting, legs crossed, on the floor of Janet's darkened room, using a Ouija board. The board itself seemed to be floating above Janet's hands. I froze. I knew something very private was happening and maybe I shouldn't be there. The Ouija board made a sudden move out of Janet's hands — and went partway across the room and fell to the floor.

The kids all said — it seemed like it was in unison — "Oh Dad!" Like I wrecked it or something. It was clear they were a group and I wasn't part of it, so I backed out and left quickly.

There were many of those "children only" Ouija board sessions, and I was to respect their privacy. They did make that clear. Since my mother was a gypsy I could understand how this all came about.

It was a wonderful memory. I think about it often.

As Janet grew up, she continued to have a keen interest in psychic abilities, and came to give Tarot card readings professionally, in recent years at upscale New York City restaurants.

She has many stories to tell as well, and a book about her experiences would be very interesting.

Peter

Peter, born in 1951, was always drawing pictures about his own cartoon characters. Some were superheroes. Some were detectives. Some were children. How I loved it when he would bring a hand-drawn story to me to read. Many were long and in great detail, and he was only seven to eight years old. I looked at one of these stories a few months ago and happily reminisced.

I remember his first date. He was 14, and we were on a week's summer vacation at the New Jersey Shore. At the beach, he made some friends with other children, in particular a pretty teenage girl.

The next thing I knew, Peter was asking for money for a date. His mother and I gulped and wondered what to do, when Peter said he wanted to take her for a bicycle ride. Much relieved, we said yes and rented two bicycles.

Peter brought his first girlfriend over to meet us, and they hopped on the two bikes and rode off. We assumed they would ride around and sightsee the town and beach.

Not a chance. When they arrived home a couple of hours later, Peter came through the door saying, "It was great! We rode all the way up to Barnegat Lighthouse and back. It was fourteen miles! It was great! And we didn't even have to stop anywhere!"

Then his date walked through the door. She was white as a sheet, and dragged her feet to the sink as she gulped two glasses of water. Still breathing hard, she said, "My God! Was it really fourteen miles? And it was nonstop, too!"

Peter was still beaming at this accomplishment, but his date was not. She wanted to go home. We took her. She was never heard from again.

Peter grew up to be a newspaper writer and editor, and his first date with his future wife, Anne, was a long bike ride. Their honeymoon was even a Vermont Bicycle Tour, which was actually Anne's idea. Not long after my ninetieth birthday, they celebrated their thirty-first wedding anniversary. Their daughter, Corinne, is a cartoonist, and their son, Alex, is working to become an actuary.

Jim

My son Jim, born in 1954, had a vibrant and positive attitude as a child. He was a Boy Scout at heart. It wasn't any wonder that he joined the Boy Scouts as soon as he was old enough. He loved the activities and the Boy Scout philosophy of being prepared and helpful.

One Christmas, we gave him a bow and arrow. He practiced and practiced until he was pretty accurate. Then one day, he came into the house shouting, "I just shot a squirrel right off the tree branch!" One of his brothers came in right behind him and added, "It hit a tree branch, and it shook so hard, the squirrel fell off it and ran away!" So much for different viewpoints.

Even more memorable was the crow story. Jim came dashing into the house, announcing he had just shot a crow that was about 100 yards away, suggesting Robin Hood-like accuracy. Then another brother walked in and added, "There were over a hundred crows in that field when he shot that arrow into them."

Jim grew up to get his doctorate in plant pathology, and teach at Florida A&M University. With his first wife, Rosa, he had two kids, Sarah, a banker, and Steve, an astrophysicist. He and his second wife, Angela, have a high-schooler named Johnny, and a little girl named Julia.

David

As the youngest, David, born in 1956, got a lot of help and attention from his brothers and sister, and he liked it. I remember this because I was the youngest, and it was fun to get the youngest child treatment. Even now the thought brings back happy memories.

David loved mechanical toys and was very good at assembling them and making them work. That leads me into the riding mower event. I asked David one day to cut the grass, using our push mower, which had no power. He did. But he complained that we didn't have a riding power mower that could cut the lawn better and faster.

I finally gave in after a heavy rain and the push mower got stuck in the wet grass. David was delighted when that riding mower arrived. He made sure all the controls worked, jumped in the seat, and took off. I smiled and said to myself, "Now he'll cut the grass." Two hours later, he walked in smiling and said, "That riding mower works great!" I rushed out to see the lawn, but the grass was still not cut. I asked him where he was the last two hours. His answer: "I won the race!"

"What race?" I asked.

"The riding mower race in the field behind our house," he said.

A small stream separated our backyard from a big field. I saw two wood planks, eight inches wide and sixteen feet long, laid across that stream.

I asked David how he got across. "I drove the riding mower across the planks," he said.

"You're crazy," I said. "Nobody could ride over those two planks safely. They would fall in the water. I don't want to see this happen again!"

That was when one of his brothers said, "Then, Dad, don't look!"

I followed that advice. I didn't look, and I never heard of any accident of the riding mower falling in the stream.

Then again, the kids didn't tell me everything.

The grass didn't get cut as often as I wanted either. But that's the way of life when you have children. You make compromises.

David grew up to use his mechanical abilities working for my business as a manufacturer's representative. He was always the one to fix things, and even to suggest improvements of various devices. His wife, Thalia, brought two daughters, Nina and Jade, to the marriage, and together, David and Thalia have a young son, Wyatt.

The grandchildren all have their own special personalities, and I have always been delighted to see them, and Carol's grandchildren, too. Carol has three children: Scotty Anderson, who is married to Marta; Steven Anderson, who is married to Monika; and Sandy, who is married to Ken Johnson. Steven's two children are Erika and Lily. Sandy's three are

Christopher, Nicholas and Kevin. The children and grandchildren have provided many, many happy times for Carol and me.

The good times I remember best. The happy memories. I can't seem to remember the problems or unhappy memories. Getting older does have something good about it, after all.

CHAPTER 19

Musical Muses

Music has always been very important to me. By the time I was in kindergarten, I had already been singing, even while walking and playing around the house. At age seven, I started singing in the junior choir at church. Now, at 90, I am still singing, and I'm the senior member in my church's senior choir, so I've been singing for more than eighty years.

In the early 1980s, a couple of years after I got married again, I lost my voice to laryngitis for about ten days. When it started to come back, to help it recover carefully, I took some voice lessons with my voice teacher, Joe Prendergast. A few weeks later, I couldn't make my voice lesson because of an Engineers Club meeting, so Joe suggested that my wife, Carol, fill in for that lesson. Carol never had a voice lesson before, but she sang over the years in her church choir. She said OK, and she did so well, Joe suggested that we take voice lessons together from then on. We did, and Joe had us singing duets in nursing homes in less than two months. Individually as singers, we were OK, but together we were better. And that became our musical way of life — playing music together and singing duets.

There is no way I could have done it by myself. Carol has been playing the piano since she was a child, and is very good with several musical instruments, especially in selecting the right chords to play and knowing how to make those necessary key changes as our voices grew older and lower. She also has an ability to chat and charm the audience and make them feel comfortable. She is a natural as a master of ceremonies in our gigs in nursing homes.

That's why I call her "my Sweetheart of Song."

As a duo, Carol and I call ourselves "The Musical Muses." We play the old-time tunes, Gospel songs, folk songs, funny songs.

We have also written more than twenty songs with lyrics. And many an evening has been spent just playing and singing music together. Some of these sessions we call "rehearsals," and a lot of what we do is just a musical jam.

In 2008, we played the autoharp and dulcimer and sang forty-three music gigs. By 2010, it was up to sixty. We usually played in churches (typically three songs) and in nursing homes (typically eighteen to twenty songs). We give free music lessons to those interested. We sometimes even loan them an autoharp for a month, but, no, we do not sell instruments. Over the years, we also played the dulcimer and autoharp in the Greater Pinelands Dulcimer Society, under the leadership of Rich and Mary Carty, who were more than music teachers — they were our friends.

Every time we write a song, it comes from inspiration right then. We would keep at it until the song was written. Early one September, Carol was on the phone with her daughter, Sandy, talking about what happened with her kids those first three days of school. I was reading the sports section, but I kept listening. After about 10 minutes, I got up, went to the computer, put on my music writing program, and started to write a song about school's first three days.

Forty-five minutes later, when I walked into the kitchen, Carol was just hanging up. "What's that?" she asked, looking at a sheet of paper in my hands. I replied, "I listened to you two talking about those first three days of school and wrote a song." I sang it to her, and "School Is in Session" has been in our songbook ever since. That forty-five minutes was my fastest time of writing a complete four-verse song with music.

Here's the chorus:

School is in session,
And the kids are learning quick.
You can't tell what they'll bring home.
You do not get your pick.

That's right. One of them brought home the flu. Carol just laughed and laughed. Then she called Sandy back and had me sing the song over the phone. Over the years, whenever we played and sang for the children in their school at Christmastime, we would always get the request to sing "School Is in Session."

Another song we wrote was "Company Is Coming and We're Not Ready Yet!" It's a house-cleaning song. Once, while on vacation in England, we were attending a concert by the Copper Family Singers, an English folk song group. My wife's maiden and married name is Carol Copper, and they called for us to sing a song. So, right after the intermission, we were introduced and sang "Company Is Coming and We're Not Ready Yet!" We did it a cappella, because we didn't have our instruments on vacation with us. The audience loved it. We got a big hand. It was a pleasant surprise for us to be asked to sing as part of the Copper Family Singers Concert.

The song's refrain goes like this:

Once a year! Once a year!
We've got to clean the house, my dear!
Company is coming, and we're not ready yet!
    (Ring a bell or simulate door chimes with high chords)
Company is coming, and we're not ready yet!

Audiences like simple catchy songs about everyday life, and we have fun singing them, too. One of Carol's favorites is "Cat on Your Feet." The first verse goes like this: "It's hard to go to sleep with a cat on your feet, cat on your feet, cat on your feet, it's hard to go to sleep with a cat on your feet." Then she follows "It's hard to go sleep" with "when the laundry is not done!" or "when the moon is shining bright and the parrot talks all night!" Sometimes, it's a dog, a squirrel or mouse "on your feet." The last verse ends with "And now what shall we do?"

When the weather's bad, we can really get an audience to

respond to another easy song. First verse: "You've got snow! We've got snow! Anybody you know want more snow?" Then everybody shouts, "No!" Other lines, like "Streets are icy and sleet's on the feet" and "The snow's as high as an elephant's eye," are all followed by "Anybody you know want more snow? No!"

CHAPTER 20

Just for Laughs: Some Favorite Jokes

I have always loved jokes, telling them and hearing them. At age 90, I'm afraid I may have forgotten some really good ones. But here's a bunch, including a few my son Jim helped me remember.

A husband and wife were celebrating their 60th birthdays, when a genie suddenly appeared. "Amazing!" said the genie. "A husband and wife born on the same day! I'm granting each of you a wish." He asked the wife, "What is your wish?" She replied, "I've always wanted to go on a round-the-world cruise." The genie said, "Your wish is granted," and the woman found herself on a ship at sea going around the world. The genie turned to the husband and asked, "What is your wish?" The husband replied, "I've always wanted a wife who was 30 years younger than me." The genie then said, "Your wish is granted. You are now 90 years old."

Late one night, a little old lady came home only to find a burglar in the house. She tiptoed behind him then yelled in her sternest voice, "Stop thief! I give you Acts 2:38! Thou shall not steal, especially from a little old lady! Now, stand still while I call the cops." She called 911, and the police arrived right away. As an officer slapped on the handcuffs, he asked the crook, "Why didn't you run away? She wasn't armed." The burglar said, "Yes, she was! She said she had an ax and two .38s!"

Mama cat was walking down the sidewalk with her kittens when she saw a big dog coming toward them. She told her kittens to go hide under a bush, and they did. She walked up to the big dog, put her nose against his, and said, "Arf! Arf! Arf!" The dog got confused and ran away. The mama cat walked back to the kittens and said, "See, kids, I told you it pays to be able to speak a second language!"

A state trooper was patrolling U.S. Route 30 in New Jersey, when he noticed an old Buick going too slow. He pulled the car over and saw the driver was a little old lady. He told her she was only going 30 miles per hour, which was too slow for a highway. "You must be mistaken, officer," she said. "The last sign read 30, so I know I was doing the speed limit." The trooper said, "Lady, that was the U.S. highway number, not the speed limit." The woman said, "Oh!" Then the officer looked in the back seat and saw two other old ladies shaking with fright. "What's wrong?" he asked. They replied, "We just got off U.S. Route 95!"

A burglar breaks into a house by climbing through an open window. A parrot sitting on its perch says, "Butterfly is watching you." The burglar says, "What?" Parrot says, "Butterfly is watching you." Burglar says, "Aw, shut up, you dumb bird," and takes a step forward. Just then, the parrot turns toward a giant dog who has been quietly sitting in the shadows baring his huge drooling fangs, and says, "Sic 'em, Butterfly!"

This fellow was out of work and was walking the streets looking for a job, when he saw a zoo. That's a big place, so they should have some jobs, he thought. He went in and asked if anything was available, but the zoo manager said, "Sorry, we don't have any good jobs." The man cried, "But I'll do anything! Anything!" The manager said, "Anything?" The guy said, "Yes, anything!" The manager looked at him and said, "Well, our monkey died yesterday, and we could use somebody to wear a monkey costume and entertain the kids until we get another monkey. The job pays well." The man says, "I'll do it!" He puts on the monkey costume, and the zoo teaches him to jump up and down like a monkey, make noises like a monkey, eat and drink like a monkey, and swing like a monkey. But during his swinging lessons, he swings so hard he soars over a fence right into the lion's cage. The lion immediately roars and starts chasing. The man yells, "Help! Somebody save me!" The lion glares at him and says, "Shut up! You want to get us both fired?"

CHAPTER 21

On Growing Older

Getting older is a very gradual thing. It steadily creeps up on you over the years while you are not looking or expecting it. One day, you are aware that something is happening, and you can do very little about it. You are growing older. For years, you have gotten up from a chair with one easy push. But now, you take two pushes to get up from a chair, and ask yourself, "What is going on?" It's old age catching up to you. Last year, for me, it was two pushes. Then it became two pushes and an occasional three. Next year if it goes to three regularly, I won't be able to get up fast enough before someone is there helping me. I am not ready for that. But I won't have a choice. People are just going to be helpful to us "old folks." If you start to accept it, then you are getting closer to needing a retirement home than you think. By their late 80s, people are supposed to have a good idea of knowing how things will go. After all, by age 75, you supposedly have enough experience to have an inkling of what 80 would be like.

So, here's what I now know about reaching 90, and it is not as good as it was at age 80. No more in and out of the bathroom in a few minutes. The old equipment just doesn't work fast anymore. But try to tell that to a grandchild, and you get a blank or confused look. Their parents are more understanding.

When I was 60, I could perform many an activity in fifteen minutes. But now it takes me an hour. Over three decades, the time to do that activity went from fifteen to thirty to forty-five to sixty minutes. Yes, it took me an hour to type the above three paragraphs. And now I have to stop, because I am tired. I will write some more tomorrow. So far, writing this book has taken me two years. And that doesn't include the notes that I collected for years before. An hour-and-a-half twice a day is a full day's activity for me. It also requires two naps that are an hour to 90 minutes each. The rest of the day is used up with miscellaneous chores and things like feeding the cats, shopping, cooking, getting dressed, watching TV, rehearsing music, then playing and singing at nursing homes, churches, historic sites, and music festivals.

We also collect books to give them to children with First Book, a nonprofit organization. We also read books to children in schools with Book Mate. When we come home after any music or reading gigs, we are exhausted, and have to nap.

I wasn't always this slow. At 75, I was still able to zip along during the day, even after playing golf with our Dawn Patrol golfers, who often teed off at 5 a.m. But arthritis ended that activity when I was 79. When I saw that I wasn't able to take a normal back swing, and then would lose the grip on the club as I hit the ball, which rolled only a short distance in the fairway, that was it! I knew that golf for me was over. Even walking back to the car was starting to get tough. That's the same age I had to give up tennis.

My wife, Carol, a retired school nurse, suggested I get into a group that did in-water exercises for arthritis. Lucky me. There was a group right in a nearby town, in the Moorestown Community Center. So I joined. On the first day, I had to walk the length of the pool to reach its steps. I had to put both hands on the handrail as I walked to those steps. As I stepped down into the water, I quickly found out I liked it. The water was buoyant. The people were friendly. The instructor, Bob Kamuca, a volunteer with arthritis, started the exercises. I began by quietly saying "Ouch" many times. But it was easy to stick to the exercise program. I had good company and a good instructor. Imagine, a pool with ten to fifteen people exercising in it with quiet ouches and cheerful attitudes. After the first ten minutes, I started saying ouch less as I exercised more. My new friends with their cheerful and encouraging conversation made me feel welcome. It was a winning combination.

After approximately forty sets, the exercises were over, and I just stayed in the water doing a few of my own exercises and chatting with my new friends. When I left, I noticed that I could walk a little easier and with a little less pain. As the weeks went by, I found that even though I climbed into the water with pain, I climbed out with less. I would be able to walk in the afternoon a little easier. Could it be that the water exercises were helping? After a couple of years, it turned out to be that way. In-water exercises keep me moving with less pain. I'll keep on taking them as long as I can. Some people come in and expect to do one session and get a lot of relief. It doesn't work that way. It is not a cure. The help is very gradual. You need to keep doing it over and over to get some relief that day. Arthritis is a tough and long-term problem.

As I got older, I tended to be more forgetful. My memory just slipped a little more each year. I'm now pretty slipped out, to a point of being very forgetful. But somehow, nobody seems to mind that *Old Steve* is getting older and more forgetful. Last year, I forgot our wedding anniversary. I mean, really! I was a week late in remembering it and finally said something to my wife, Carol. And she said, "Oops! I forgot, too!" We looked at each other and started laughing to cover our joint embarrassment. How did we make up for it? Over the next month, every time one of us goofed, forgot, misinterpreted or make some other mistake, or even did or said something nice, one would look at the other and say, "Happy anniversary!" Then both would start to laugh. It's been like a game, seeing who can surprise the other with an occasion to bring out the words "Happy anniversary!" One night, as we went to bed, Carol whispered in my ear, "Happy anniversary!" (I could even call this an example of positive criticism.)

I sure liked this result better than getting a reprimand for forgetting our wedding anniversary, just because I'm getting older and more forgetful. And you know what? At my age, I don't have a choice anymore. I just have to accept it.

But at 85, you couldn't convince me. I wasn't ready yet. After all, at 85, I could still walk up and down steps without holding a handrail and could even carry two packages.

By age 87, it was one package and hold the handrail.

About 2005, I started having teeth pulled. Last year, I had two pulled, and, as of 2011, I had only eighteen of my own teeth left. But they seem to be in good shape, my dentist said.

I wonder what next year will bring.

And the year after that ... and the year after that ... if I continue to be lucky.

I saw on television an announcement that 50 percent of the people alive today could live to be 100 years old. Immediately I thought, "I could never imagine it!"

I would be broke long before that. And I didn't want to put that burden on my children. Imagine a son or daughter, 65 to 75 years old and possibly retired, trying to take care of a parent who's 90 to 100 years old. Two retirees on one budget? The child's savings might need to last another 20 to 30 years.

Medicare would throw up! Social Security would cry, "We are empty!" Where would the money come from? The answer could be from your own retirement savings.

Will you be prepared for the cost of your possibly longer future? Will you also be ready for the potential cost of adding a parent who had enough life left, but not enough money? It's scary! And it's not fair for someone who worked and saved only to learn it wasn't enough after all. Children might need to start saving in their twenties for such possibly longer retirements. Anyone who lives extra long will need more money in those extra later years.

I can't even begin to go into the multiple complexities of this problem that's just starting to show up. They are too much for a 90-year-old man. I will have to leave this tough problem to your younger minds.

I wish you good luck.

Cherish the good times, and the positive souls in your life, and, ahem, beware of ice holes.

That reminds me of a joke my kids loved when they were little. Do you know how to catch a polar bear? Well, you find a frozen lake, and using a saw, you cut a big hole in the ice. Next, you take a bag of peas and place them one by one in a ring all around the cutout. So, when a bear shows up to take a pea, you kick him in the ice hole!

Sorry, I couldn't resist.

At least, when you get old you don't have to lose your sense of humor!

About the Author

Steve Mucha, born in 1921, lived through the Great Depression as a child in the working-class town of Carteret, New Jersey. His parents came over from Czechoslovakia before meeting in the United States, getting married, and starting a family. Helping his parents run a family store and other early experiences taught him not only the wisdom of saving, but how saving could help people be generous.

Steve served in World War II and met his first wife while going to Swarthmore College to earn an engineering degree on the G.I. Bill. To help raise four children, mostly in the Philadelphia suburbs, he went from designing photographic printing equipment to selling it, then from being a sales manager to starting a business as a manufacturer's representative. He has long loved photography, golf, tennis, jokes and music. Remarriage and retirement brought lots of new adventures, including the writing of this book. He lives in Pennsauken, New Jersey, with his wife, Carol, three cats of their own, and about four neighborhood strays they feed.